THE BED DEFILED

Disharmony After Matrimony? Why?

By

SYLVIA M DALLAS

International Standard Book Numbers:
Ebook: 978-976-95691-9-5
Paperback: 978-976-95691-8-8

All biblical references are from the King James Versions (KJV) unless otherwise indicated. Quotations from The Passion Translation are indicated with the letters TPT
Quotations from New Life Translation are indicated with the letters NLT

Published by: The Publisher's Notebook Limited
email:PUBLISHER@thepublishersnotebook.com

THE PUBLISHER'S NOTEBOOK
'Envision it, we'll publish it'

DEDICATION

To the Holy Spirt for His conviction in my spirit, His guidance and His teachings.

To my husband Rohan Dallas, for your permission to write this book and understanding that I must be obedient to our God. I still say the safest place on this earth for me is in your arms.

To Deacons Lloyd and Lorraine Patterson, for your eager anticipation of this book.

To Pastor Courtney Morrision, for giving me the forum to present this book.

To Pastor Richard McCarthy for your critique and for holding me accountable.

To the members of the Feltab family who upheld me in prayer throughout the trials I experienced while writing this book.

To Carol Henry who keeps "chatting to God about me"

To Vivienne, Sodene, Yolanda, Letisha, Violet who uphold me in prayer

To my beta readers – who gave valuable feedback

To my "big brothers" - Rowan Wade, Hubert Lawrence, Michael Dixon and David Laylor, thanks for the male perspective.

Lastly, to the couples to whom this book
will minister, PRESS IN, PRESS ONWARD,
DO NOT EVER GIVE UP!

Sylvia M Dallas

TABLE OF CONTENTS

FOREWORD

This masterpiece entitled "The Bed Defiled" is an eight chapter, one hundred and forty-one pages Thesis on the subject of marriage from God's stand point.

Sylvia demonstrates her unashamed yet inspiring personal expose from the crucible of a great slice of her life, demonstrating strengths and weaknesses we can learn from today.

Some in The Body of Christ are wonderful preachers, others teachers of God's Word and some are excellent writers, but the author has distinguished herself in all these areas.

In this book we are brought back to the altar to observe Christ and His love relationship with the Church, His own Bride, as the romantic warrior, and the lover of lovers.

The use of scripture and their in-depth meaning and content all point to God. The argument for Holiness and Righteousness from the worshiper, highlights that our lives are not our own, but we are temples of the living God. 1Cor. 3:16

Some of the challenges that are highlighted are ones that pastors, families, men and women, face within and without our churches. Many hide from these issues, but Sylvia faces them head on.

The reader will laugh and will cry, will be confronted and challenged but it will be for the purpose of change and bringing one to Christlikeness.

Bishop Neville Owens
Love and Faith World Outreach Ministries
http://www.loveandfaith.org

PREFACE

I have been very concerned about the growing rate of divorce in the church, which is considered by many to be alarming. From whichever perspective you view marriage, the institution of marriage Christian or otherwise, is in trouble. Why is this so?

The simple and most obvious reason is that it is an institution ordained by God and therefore Satan will oppose it with all his might. Satan is always opposed to the will of God.

The high rate of divorce, particularly in the church, has been such a concern that it is partly the reason that some people decide to live together - the fear of the process of marriage not working. The media also has been responsible for sensationalizing the divorce process - especially of celebrities. Too often, we see nasty custody fights, dirty laundry being aired and a myriad of other distasteful displays that just cement in our minds that marriage is not for us.

I came to that conclusion after the end of my first marriage. I forgave my ex-husband (and no, the fault was not only his), and to this day we have maintained a good friendship. I swore that I would never get married again. So did my current husband. Thank God for deliverance. We both made a decision to fight to make it work, without even understanding the principle behind the decision. It was not just based on the love we share. We believe that God ordained us to be together.

As you progress throughout this book, you will be made aware of some things that happened in my marriage, which caused me to ask the Father - "Why is this happening?" "How come this was not happening when we were living together?" "Is it that we are wrong for each other?" "Are we going to be another divorce statistic?" "Are we being punished for something?" It is not easy to open up my life like this, but I made a promise to be obedient to God no matter how hard it is for me.

Thankfully, after a period of questioning Him and deliverance experiences for my husband and I, He has answered.

I experienced a level of discomfort with this book. The Lord plainly told me, that I would have to reveal things that happened in my marriage. Can you picture the scene when He said that to me? I sat on the chair, turned to the side and pouted. For almost one hour all I said was "No. No. No," shaking my head and arguing that there must be another way to write this book. I remember going to my husband, explaining this mandate from the Lord and seeking his permission to do this book, promising to be discreet. He agreed that I should do it. (So much for my "out"). The patient Holy Spirit just simply waited for me to submit to His will, and I did with much grieving in my heart as I knew that my life would be an open book after this.

I expect that this book will be cathartic to some extent, for me and for you. It will involve facing some ugly truths about ourselves, admitting some wrongs and righting them. It will be painful but remedial. It must bring freedom.

Prayer

Father in Heaven, I thank You for instilling in me the courage to write this book. Because of my obedience to You, I had to face issues in my life that I would otherwise ignore. By the power of Your Word, I have been delivered, and traps around my mind have been sprung. I pray for the married couples and those planning to get married who read this book, that it will minister to them and that they may experience healing in their lives and their relationship. May Your Name be glorified by this work, in Jesus' precious name, Amen.

THE

BED

DEFILED

Disharmony after Matrimony? Why?

Sylvia M Dallas

Chapter One: Single, Alone, Lonely - Are they the same?

Oftentimes these three terms are used to mean the same thing, but nothing could be further from the truth.

One of these terms speaks of uniqueness, another of being isolated, and the other of being in a negative emotional state. In order to better understand their meanings and applications let's look at their definitions in both the Hebrew and English.

Before the first surgery in history was performed, Adam was a single man. As a matter of fact, he was one (single), divided, and then one (united with Eve) again.

Being Single

Definition

Single -unique, unaccompanied, alone, solo, unattached, free, individual[1]

Single comes from the Hebrew word ecadh[2] which refers to the uniqueness of God.

I never understood the term "singleness" until recently when I attended Bible College.[3] As I listened to Apostle Al Miller expound on the topic of being single, I experienced a growing sense of alarm about my marriage. Once he started to expound on the meaning of single, I realized to my dismay, that neither Rohan nor I were single in the true sense of the Word when we got married.

When I met my husband, I was a Christian, although I was not walking the walk. I rationalized everything about the Bible to fit my life, instead of adjusting

---

[1] http://dictionary.com
[2] Www.ichthys.com/mail-Hebrew%20word%20for%20one.htm
[3] Whole Life College & Leadership Institute

3

my life to accommodate the fulfillment of the Word.

During the four and a half years we lived together outside of the sanctity of marriage, we rarely quarreled, we got along just fine. We went hiking together, had adventures together. I was often at sea with him or in the bush camping with him as he hunted wild boar. It was as if we were joined at the hip. As we settled into our regular lives (I did have customers to attend to), we got used to our times of not being together all the time. It never bothered us. I understood that he was doing his hunting and fishing long before I came on the scene, and he understood that I had my clients to attend to. After all we were doing these things before we met.

What is singleness? It is the ability to stand alone. It is not to be confused with loneliness. Being single means standing financially, spiritually, emotionally and all the other ' -ally's" that come at us in our daily walk in life. We must be able to do without the crutches and stand without falling. This means that someone who smokes, cannot do without sex, cannot be alone etc, is not single. Singleness is the time to deal with our emotional baggage and the destructive habits that we have developed. The period of singleness teaches self-control.

It is also the time to develop healthy relationships and give of yourself wholly to the Kingdom of God. The period of singleness is not a time to be idle but it is a period of preparation.

As I said before, Rohan and I had gotten married, but we were not single at the time of getting married. In addition to the struggles we faced in our marriage the primary reason being the focus of this book, we had to deal with a lot of emotional and spiritual issues. It would have been easier if we were single first.

It bears repeating - Adam was a single man. He was unique (in the image and likeness of God[4]), he was working (tending the garden[5]), he had no emotional baggage, he could provide for and protect a wife (he had dominion[6]

---

[4] Genesis 1:26,27,
[5] Genesis 2:15
[6] Genesis 1:28

over the entire Garden, he was healthy (not dependent on any drugs, only on God). He was in a relationship with God[7], was giving himself wholly to the Kingdom of God, and had not developed any destructive habits.

Being Alone

Definition

Alone - separate, apart, isolated from others[8]

We see from Genesis 1 through to Genesis 2:17 - that everything that God makes, He says is "good". Here in verse 18 is the first time we see where God says something is "not good". "It is not good that man should be alone [separate, apart, isolated from others]".

Marriage was not ordained by God to solve the problem of loneliness, it was meant to solve the problem of aloneness –Apostle Al Miller. God said, "it is not

---

[7] Genesis 3:5
[8] Dictionary.com

good that the man should be alone; I will make him an help meet[9] for him[10]".

The word 'meet' used here is the Hebrew word ezer (ay-zer) whose root is azar (aw-zar) which means to surround, that is, protect or aid: - help, succor.

The man must reach the stage in his life where he recognizes that in his singleness, he no longer wants to be alone.

A common misconception is that women are the "weaker sex". Right away we see in the definition of help "meet" that the woman is supposed to help support, protect and surround the man.

"I will make him an help meet for him"

Why does that verse have that sentence structure? In the subsequent verses, we see where Adam named all the animals and we see where it was said that "*but for Adam there was not found an help meet for him*"[11]. Why was this said after

---

[9] Ultimate Bible Study Suite - Strong's 05826
[10] Genesis 2:18 KJV
[11] Genesis 2:20 KJV

all the animals were named? Did God not know already that there was not a help meet for Adam? That could not be the case because we see in verse 18, that God had already recognized that Adam was alone and needed a help meet. I believe that God caused Adam to name all the animals first so that he (Adam) could see that there was no help meet for him among the animals.

At this point Adam recognized and understood that he was alone, and I believe that this birthed a desire for companionship in him.

When the relationship between Rohan and I became sexual, we were not living together at the time. As far as I was concerned, we were "together". One day he said to me "I'm going to make certain of you. I'm giving you my name". It took me two days to realize I was being proposed to. I called him and asked "Did you propose to me?" He answered "Yes". I said "Okay then" after which he asked me what that meant. (Well, he's not the only one that can be cryptic). Soon after he handed me a key, made space in his chest of drawers and told me to come home. Now engaging in sexual relations with him and subsequently moving in with him was not my best decision as a Christian (walking in rebellion or not), but that's the truth of it.

The long and short of it was that he no longer wanted to be alone and neither did I, but we were not single. He had his crutches - smoking, hanging on the corner with his friends until late, etc., and I lacked self-control. I had a foul temper, was emotional and cried easily. I was frightened because I allowed myself to become vulnerable with him. Because of my temper, to this day, I do not have a single glass vase, or any mirrors except for a tiny piece left in the wardrobe door. *(I think it is really about time I remedied that).* Thankfully these episodes did not happen regularly, but when they did - epic proportions. We settled into a routine and lived harmoniously for the most part.

Being Lonely

Definition
Lonely - affected with, characterized by, or causing a depressing feeling of being[12]

Here in the very definition of the word we see the difference between **alone** and **lonely**. One recognizes the need for companionship, and the other, recognizing the same need, becomes depressed about it.

In an effort to stave off loneliness, we engage in activities that we have no business participating in. These activities include and are not limited to - comfort eating, drinking alcohol, over working, sexual involvement.

It is a spiritually unhealthy state to be dependent on self and not on God. Loneliness has a "me" focus. Loneliness in a marriage, if not dealt with, leads to either spouse desperate to find a connection to ease the pain in their hearts. One of the causes of loneliness in a marriage comes from not being

---

[12] Http://dictionary.com

single before marriage. Lonely people do not know how to stand alone. I do not believe that people who take part in extra marital affairs (with the exception of a minority), actually plan to end up in sexual affairs. It seems to start out innocently enough. First, the spouse who feels wronged, finds an ear to vent to about their marriage, primarily because they have reached a stage where they feel that they are unable to communicate with their partner. Then the attraction subtly creeps in. Remember – subtlety is the hallmark of the devil.

Before long, he/she finds themselves spilling all the beans about their marriage and eventually this person becomes the "run to" person when anything goes wrong. Next thing you know, hugs, lending a shoulder to cry on, stroking/comforting touches are administered, an "innocent kiss" all lead to the intense physical sexual connection. The border has been crossed and instead of repenting and correcting the situation, they surrender to the "this feels right" deception of the enemy. The whole thing comes down to

"I need to feel good/accepted/validated."
It is no longer about your covenant with
God and your spouse.

I remember telling Rohan once that I
was lonely. He responded by telling me
that I cannot be lonely and married.
Fortunately, I recognized that my
husband believes that now that we are
married, there is nothing much that he
has to do. In the same way, there are
people who believe that accepting Jesus
Christ as their Lord and Saviour is the
end all and be all of their salvation
experience. I have tried to dissuade him
of this belief, to no avail. I leave that
particular job to the Holy Spirit.

Recognizing my vulnerability, I became
aware of all kinds of temptations coming
at me to alleviate the loneliness. Thank
God for the Holy Spirit. The first thing
the Holy Spirit cautioned me against was
speaking about the marital problems to
(a) people who were single (b) people
who were divorced [especially those who
were still bitter] and (c) my male friends.
Well, that narrowed down the field
somewhat. I have a few friends that I
can confide in and ask them to keep my

marriage in prayer, and there is a broader group that I can say "hey, keep my marriage in prayer" without ever having to give details.

What to do with those empty nights? I eventually learned to stop focusing on the loneliness and actively sought to deepen my relationship with God. I also use the time to write. When Rohan is home, I put down all writing, even if he is sleeping. The deepening of my relationship with God has enabled me to stay faithful in my marriage. I could have reasoned that he was leaving me alone at nights and I was lonely so I had to have companionship. As a matter of fact, it had been subtly suggested to me, I would be justified in my actions should I so choose to do. Needless to say, that person is now on the list of persons whom I love from afar. There are times when you have to examine your friendships and determine if they are good for your marriage. Once you make the determination that their "medicine is wrong", that they are toxic to your relationship, you have to purpose to keep them as far away from your marriage as possible. I am not saying that you should act with malice towards them, or not speak to them, but you cannot maintain a close relationship with them for the sake and safety of your marriage.

I heard one of my favorite ministers, Rev Jesse Duplantis, said once "It's not about what you feel, but what the Word of God says." As long as what I feel does not match up with the Word of God, then the Word of God wins - no contest.

In summary, loneliness takes our focus from God and gives way to feelings of depression that lead us into unrighteous acts, even suicide. It is actually a very selfish emotion. It is all about how I feel, what I am going to do to make myself feel better and it does not matter who gets hurt in the process. This "me" focus is devilish and focusing on self, was never how God intended us to be. Can you imagine Jesus on the road to Calvary saying "Father, I cannot manage this, it does not make me feel good and these people are too wicked anyway. Let them die". What a mess!!

When you focus on yourself only, it takes your focus from God. Anything that takes your focus from God has become an idol and He has said that we should have no other gods before Him.[13]

---

[13] Exodus 20:3

Chapter Two: Getting Married? What's Your Motive?

Too often the motive for getting married is wrong. For some (both men and women) it is usually to have a stable home, to have financial security, for the sake of the children, a misconstrued idea of love, to escape a situation, or to end loneliness. None of these motives are correct.

What follows is a questionnaire that I wrote as I was listening to Apostle Al Miller, the president of Whole Life Bible College & Leadership Institute lecture on the topic of "Choosing a Mate". In summary, the man must be ready to end his aloneness and the woman must be ready to be a help meet to her spouse.

Questionnaire For The Man

1. Do I know God?
2. Do I know my purpose and the will of God for my life?
3. Am I pursuing my purpose?
4. What is my vision?
5. Am I committed to the principle of work?
6. Am I doing something for which I require help?
7. Am I ready for responsibility?
8. Do I have a dependency?
9. Have I dealt with the issues of my childhood?
10. Am I alone or just lonely?
11. Am I ready to not be alone anymore?
12. Can this woman solve my aloneness problem?
13. Will she stick with me?
14. Is she my friend?
    a. Does she have the qualities of a friend?
    b. What do I consider most important in a friend?
15. Can I trust her?
    a. Does she demonstrate trustworthiness?
    b. Can I bank on her support?
    c. Does she enjoy being around me?
    d. Do I enjoy being around her?
    e. Am I fulfilled?
    f. Does she excite me?
    g. Can we talk?
16. Can she help me fulfill my purpose?

17. Is she committed to my purpose?
18. What is her purpose?
    a. Will she be able to fulfill her purpose while helping me?
19. Does she have the attitude and spirit of an helper?
    a. Is she teachable?
    b. Is she supportive?
    c. Is she submissive?
    d. Is she suitable?
    e. A natural fit?
    f. Adaptable?
30 Am I able to meet her needs?
31 Seek her best welfare?
32 Will she allow me?
33 Will she be an help or a strain?
34 Will she be a good mother?
35 Can I be one with her?
    a. Can we merge?
    b. Is there enough likeness to create oneness?
36 Is she willing to be honest, truthful and open without shame?
37 Is she reflecting the image of God?
38 Does she understand and is she willing to serve the mandates of Dominion and Redemption?

Questionnaire For The Woman

1. Do I know God?
2. What is my purpose and the will of God for my life?
3. Am I pursuing my purpose?

4. What is my vision?
5. Is my understanding of my role in marriage aligned with the Word of God?[14]
6. Am I willing to submit to his authority?
7. Do I have a desire to care for him and children?
8. Have I learned how to keep a home?
9. Is this man in the image and likeness of God?
10. Is he exercising his dominion?
11. Does he recognize me as bone of his bones?
12. Will he treat me as part of himself?
13. Does he see me as necessary and essential to the completion of his mission?
14. Is he ready to lose himself in humility to create oneness?
15. Is he ready (mature and functional) to leave and cleave to me?
16. Is he willing to be open, truthful and honest without shame?
17. What is my role as his wife to be?
18. Is he alone?
19. Does he recognize his aloneness and no longer wants to be alone?
20. Can I satisfy his aloneness needs?
21. Is he looking for a companion?
22. Can I stick with him 24/7 because he must never be alone again?
23. Does he see me as his friend?
    a. What constitutes a friend?

---

[14] Genesis 2:18-25, Proverbs 31

b. Does he enjoy being around me?
   c. Can we talk freely and openly?
   d. Do we trust each other?
   e. Does he value my opinion?
   f. Does he value my presence?
24. Can I help him?
   a. What is he doing that needs help?
   b. What is his purpose?
   c. When I help him will I enjoy helping him?
25. What is my purpose?
26. When I help him to fulfill his purpose, will it enable me to fulfill my purpose?
27. Is he "helpable"?
28. Do I suit him?
29. Am I adaptable?
30. Will he make a good father / leader?
31. Would I want my children to be like him?
32. Do we agree on the fundamental issues of life?
33. Can I become one with this man?

I encourage you to prayerfully consider these questions and ask the Holy Spirit to help you to sort out the ones that you are unable to answer, especially if you are already married.

Chapter Three: Dealing With Fear

Without a doubt, fear is the most crippling tool used by the enemy against us. Fear prevents us from achieving our divine purpose. Fear negates our faith in God. In other words, it is the opposite of faith. Hebrews 11:6 says that "without faith it is impossible to please God", therefore giving in to fear causes us to disobey and displease God.

When we look at circumstances and listen to outside influences instead of seeking the face of God and choosing to listen to His Words, the result is that we end up seeing mountains. Mountains look large, insurmountable, dangerous and sometimes not worth the effort.

The Bible is replete with encouragement and exhortation not to give in to fear. In fact, we are told that the fearful are among those who shall have their part in the lake of fire.

That is not cool - pun intended. Fear is a tool that the devil uses to make us walk in disobedience to the will of God. Fear causes us to oppose the will of God for our lives. Before you know it, you are doing the "can't bother echo".

There are some people who will not accept salvation because they fear that they will slip up, that they will not get it right. They have completely missed the real message of Grace.

Even as I write this section, my mind is beset with fear. What if I write about my marriage as a success only to have it fail? What if I speak about my husband's faithfulness only to be presented with proof that he has been unfaithful all this time? What if? What if? More "what if" questions come to my mind than an Excel[1] spreadsheet. I also find myself asking questions about his whereabouts that I would not normally ask. When he calls me to tell me that he did not bother to go to sea because the weather changed, I want to ask "So why didn't you come

---

[1] Excel is a registered trademark of Microsoft Corp.

home? Where did you sleep? And with who?" I have refused to voice these questions to Rohan. He will know soon enough when I read this book to him.

I recognized that these questions came into my thoughts the minute that I committed to finishing this book and publish it by November 2015.

As far as I am concerned, the answer to the questions is simply, "I will have to deal with that in prayer". That does not mean that I will not feel hurt and have to deal with forgiveness issues that will arise, if those fears come true. I have simply decided that I will not be crippled by fear. I am not owning this fear and calling it "my fear". My job is to be obedient to God regardless of what the enemy throws at me. I figure that whatever arises, if any, God is more than capable of dealing with it. Fear, in any form, is best dealt with by prayer and declaring the Word of God in the situation.

Testimony

While writing this book, I have experienced intimidation on a level like never before. I mean, apart from the questions that bombarded my mind about Rohan, there have been near death experiences. In one week, for example, I nearly walked into a bus three times. Now I never distract myself when crossing the road or driving, but these buses just seemed to appear out of nowhere while I was crossing. Hello!!! These are big yellow buses, too big not to see! The following week, I was crossing the road to go to church. In light of what happened the previous week, I was extra careful to look twice before crossing the road. As I was about to step off the sidewalk, I heard the Holy Spirit tell me not to move, so naturally I stayed put. Suddenly, a car came around the corner at top speed and careened up the road.

Until that time, I never thought much about how important this book must be. A day later, a friend of mine messaged me and told me that he did not know what book I was working on but God gave me a message to deliver and he was standing in prayer with me.

The Holy Spirit reminded me of a vision that I had while at a prayer retreat in December 2013. I saw the following:

1. Waves crashing on the sea shore
2. A tall palm waving in a strong wind
3. A huge boulder out in the sea - like a small island made entirely of rock
4. Sheltered cove - safe harbour
5. I can see the wind

This vision describes exactly what I am experiencing now. Seeing the wind was especially strange. I do not mean that I could see the effects of the wind, I could actually see the wind. When I asked the Holy Spirit what that meant, He told me that I would see the enemy clearly, not just the effects of the enemy's devices.

Every time that I am tempted to feel fearful, I remember this and thank God for my Rock, my safe harbour which is Jesus Christ.

Fear – Of Man

Proverbs 29:25 Fear of man will prove to be a snare, but whoever trusts in the LORD is kept safe **(NIV)**

Fear and intimidation is a trap that holds you back, but place your confident trust in the Lord and you will be seated in the high place! **(TPT)**

How often have we heard ourselves say "I wonder if they will think I am stupid?" Or, "I wonder what so and so will think if I do this." Especially for Christians, this often comes up when we are prompted by the Holy Spirit to do something outside of our comfort zone. Sometimes our reaction is "people are going to think that I am weird" or some such thought, and then we move in disobedience to the prompting of the Holy Spirit.

As it says in the above scripture, fear of man is a snare to us. A snare is a trap, something to harm us or bring us to death. The internet abounds with stories of men and women who have missed the ones that were chosen of God for them because they did not match up to their ideal. Afraid of what their society would

26

think, they only saw the person in their present circumstance and could not look beyond that. Seeing these persons years later, they see what they missed, if only...

Some of these stories are urban legends, but they are usually based on a nugget of fact.

Sometimes we get involved sexually with people who were meant to be our friends - nothing more. These people were not meant to be our spouse. They were meant to be in our lives for a season, possibly to help us over a hurdle or work out something in us. As a matter of fact, we should not be involved sexually with anyone until after marriage. Often, realizing our mistake, we stay in the relationship because we would rather not admit our error. What would our friends think? Would they laugh? Did they see this all along? How are we going to face them after this? Here is the trap: **"better to stay and tough it out."** This leads to a life that depicts happiness on the surface, but with an underbelly of misery. We end up living a lie instead of living in truth.

There are times when peer pressure causes us to get involved in a sexual relationship when we would rather not. Yes, peer pressure is not just for youngsters, seemingly mature adults succumb to it too. Succumbing to this kind of pressure, causes us to compromise our standards, in this case, of holiness and purity.

If we trust in the Lord and not worry about what people think, but obey His word and walk in His way, we are assured of the selection of the right person for us when we are ready to handle the commitment of marriage.

Declaration:

Father in Heaven, I declare that as of this day, I fear only You and not man. I acknowledge that the fear of man is a trap to me, but I will be exalted because I trust only in You. I know that You Lord are for me and are my helper, and man can do nothing to me[15]. I know it is better to take refuge in you than to trust in man.[16]Even better Lord, I know that

---

[15] Psalm 118:6, Hebrews 13:6
[16] Psalm 118:8

you did not give me a spirit of fear, but of love power and a disciplined mind[17]. Thank You for your perfect love which casts out all fear.[18] In the name of Jesus, I declare that this to be a truth for my life. Amen.

Fear - Failure/Commitment

Proverbs 2:6-8 – He plans success for the decent and honorable; he guards the course and protects the way of his faithful ones

A lot of people are reluctant to get married because of the fear of failing. This fear tends to come upon people who have experienced the pain of their parents getting divorced. It also affects, persons who have seen their married parents quarrel incessantly, have physical fights, and inflict verbal abuse on each other. Perhaps they have been born out of wedlock, seeing their parents live in harmony, but as soon as they get married, all hell breaks loose. Whatever the experience, fear takes a firm grip on

---

[17] 1 Timothy 1:7
[18] 1 John 4:18

them and they vow "I am never getting married." By making this vow, they have entered into a covenant with fear. Eventually they meet someone and are willing to live together, believing that they have an "out" if things do not work out. The minute a problem arises, they disappear.

When there is a commitment to marriage, to the "till death do us part" - there is a willingness to work through the problems. There is an emotional investment that is not easy to ignore or discard. There is a willingness to forgive and to let go. When this commitment exists, we resist the urge to cut and run, even if that was our habit in previous relationships. We are more likely to pray our way through a problem, seek counseling, or do whatever it takes to get it right.

A common lie of the enemy is that we are not committed when we are cohabiting outside of marriage. The longer a couple stays together, the more likely it is that they will purchase a house, furniture, a vehicle, have children and even go into business together. Is this not commitment? Therefore a grand deception is taking place. These couples have been duped into living a less than honorable life before God, because of fear.

We have to apply the word of God to every issue of fear that comes up on our life.

Declaration

My Father, I thank You that my mind is blessed and I have the mind of Christ[19]. You are my God who counsels me[20]. Your excellent Spirit is upon me[21], through You I have understanding, therefore, I can do all things through Christ who enables me[22]. I appropriate Your promise for good success, when I choose Your way, walk in Your Word, and not deviating from Your Word looking neither left nor right. I declare this to be a truth for my life in the name of Jesus. Amen.

---

[19] 1 Corinthians 2:17

[20] Psalm 16:7

[21] Daniel 6:3

[22] Phillippians 4:13

Fear - Success

I know that this is strange one. Why would anyone fear success? I admit I was a bit baffled on this one, so I went searching the internet to see if I could find anything written on the subject. I found an excellent article written by Pastor Blaine Smith, the author of **The Yes Anxiety: Taming the Fear of Commitment in Relationships, Career, Spiritual Life and Daily Decisions (Damascus, Maryland, USA, Silver Crest Books, 2011).** He was generous enough to give me permission to reproduce the article in this book. I am of the opinion that it handles the subject of the **Fear of Success** quite adequately.

Facing Your Fears of Success
And Finding the Courage To Let Your Light Shine

*When working on my first book, **Knowing God's Will**, I labored under the typical apprehensions of a writer--that I might not finish the project or find a suitable publisher if I did. But while my fear of failing was significant, I worried as much about what would happen if I* *succeeded! Writing a book means casting something of your private life and thought before the public, and that's scary. Would friends who liked me in my present role still like me in my new one?*

And did God himself want me to succeed? Perhaps I didn't deserve to have a published book. Perhaps he would punish me for seeking this level of accomplishment.

I recognize now that my anxieties about success were not unusual, nor merely the fate of those who write, but the experience of many in every type of pursuit. Psychologists have shown considerable interest in this area of personal conflict, which they've dubbed "the fear of success." As specialists in the field never tire in pointing out, the fear of success is not the same as the fear of failure, not just a misstatement of the latter. The fear of failure is the apprehension that you'll never reach your goal. The fear of success is being afraid that you will reach it but suffer disaster as a result. While the two fears are related in many obvious ways, they are distinct.

Specialists observe too that while the fear of success paralyzes some, we all experience it to some degree. The fear is often unconscious, revealing itself in dreams and otherwise inexplicable acts of self-sabotage. An aunt of mine bailed out of a four-year college program only two weeks before graduation. Although her grades were good and only a few assignments remained, she claimed she had lost interest in getting the degree and saw no purpose in finishing. This was an extreme example of the fear of success at work.

Yet often the fear shows up in more subtle forms of self-defeat: a migraine forcing you to cancel a cherished date; laryngitis before a vocal performance; shutting the door on a finger before a violin recital; staying up late and exhausting yourself the night before an important exam; forgetting where you put a vital document; coming down with the flu shortly after you begin an exercise program; getting an eye infection halfway through a writing project; backing a new car into a fire hydrant; taking too long to pack and missing the train; working too hard on a project and wearing yourself out.

A Special Problem for Christians
Christians unquestionably are more prone to this fear than most people. Christian teaching often fails to balance biblical perspectives on the evils of the desires of the flesh and the need for self-denial, with the positive role of motivation and accomplishment in the Christian life. The result is a myriad of success phobics among modern Christians. Many Christians are convinced God doesn't wish them to enjoy significant success. There seems to be more nobility and humility in failure--and much less hazard to your relationship with Christ!

Scripture offers plenty of warnings about the potential dangers of success. Yet it speaks just as often about the positive side of success and the importance of using our gifts constructively for God's glory. "Whatever he does prospers," the first psalm declares of the godly person (v. 3). God has ordained each of our lives to certain accomplishment. Yet the fear of success can hold us back from God's best as greatly as any other inhibition or sin.

Peter's Example

We find an enlightening example of the fear of success in one of the early encounters that Peter and his friends had with Jesus, described in Luke 5:1-11. They had fished all night yet caught nothing. Jesus tells them to drop their nets once again, and this time their catch is so huge that they can scarcely haul it ashore. Peter then declares to Jesus, "Depart from me, for I am a sinful man, O Lord" (v. 8).

We would have expected Peter and his friends to be elated over their unexpected triumph. Such an overwhelming catch of fish is a fisherman's dream. They surely would want Jesus to give them this success again and again.

Instead, they were taken drastically off guard by this sudden, inexplicable feat. They had grown accustomed to failure, and success was a jolt to their comfort zone. They felt morbidly unworthy of it. They undoubtedly feared that as Jesus came to know them better, he would judge them fraudulent and use this same miraculous power to destroy them.

Jesus, in magnanimous compassion and grace, ignored Peter's self-defeating request (thank God he often ignores our misguided prayers). He assured Peter and his friends that he intended more success for them, and on a more meaningful level. "Don't be afraid; from now on you will catch men" (v. 10). His response clearly calmed the disciples' fears. They were so relieved to find he had positive intentions for them that "they pulled their boats up on shore, left everything and followed him" (v. 11).

I'm certain that high among Jesus' greatest healing miracles was giving his early followers victory over their fears of success. He inspired within them the spiritual and psychological strength to bound beyond the inertia of their routine existence into the dynamic life of following him. In Peter the change was nothing short of revolutionary. On the day of Pentecost this man who had been plagued with inferiority stood up and forcefully addressed the multitude, convincing many to repent and follow Christ. Later, even the Jewish authorities were astonished "when they saw the courage of Peter and John and realized that they were unschooled, ordinary men" (Acts 4:13).

If you're fearful of success, take heart. You're not alone. This is an area of struggle for many. Christ understands your predicament. As surely as he has saved you, he can give you the grace to overcome this fear and realize your full potential for him.

Characteristics of the Fear of Success
Let's look more closely at what characterizes the fear of success. There are certain common anxieties that many experience in anticipation of reaching a goal.

❏**The fear of punishment from God**. *Some fear that God won't be pleased if they succeed in reaching a long-cherished goal. He surely knows they aren't worthy of this success. It will mean experiencing more pleasure and happiness than they're entitled to. Accomplishing their objective will make them more competitive with God, more like God. He won't like it. He will punish them.*

The fear of being punished by God for succeeding, while obviously related to our spiritual perspective, seems also to be rooted in our psychological heritage. Many primitive societies have rituals of sacrifice established for appeasing the gods when one realizes personal success. And dream therapy reveals that confirmed atheists have subconscious fears of retribution from a God they consciously deny exists.

*❏**The fear of losing others' affection.** Another common fear is that others will love you less if you reach your goal. The complexes producing this fear can run deep and sometimes originate in childhood. If your parents constantly criticized you and belittled your chances of succeeding at anything, you may feel uncomfortable now defying their negative expectations. Your success would be a blow to their esteem, a snub of their judgment. You worry about the effect of wounding their pride-- would they think less of you or withdraw their affection?*

Even if your childhood experience has not inclined you to fear losing others' affection through succeeding, it is still natural to worry about how others will react to your success. Friends have grown accustomed to you and appreciate you as you are now. Their personal identify may even have a stake in your not changing. Will they be offended if you succeed? Will they esteem you less? Such worries are common and stifle many from taking the steps needed to realize their potential.

*❏**The fear of outdoing others**. We may also feel uneasy about succeeding in an area where*

a family member or close friend has failed. Our success might cause them to feel the pain of their failure even more, we imagine, and so we fear hurting them. Even if this person is rooting for us to succeed, we may still feel it's inappropriate to allow ourselves to enjoy a benefit they failed to attain.

In her mammoth fifteen-year study of the effects of divorce on children, Judith Wallerstein observes that women whose mothers suffered a failed marriage often feel guilty availing themselves of a good opportunity to marry. It isn't fair to let themself enjoy bliss that life failed to serve up to mom.

While men may hold back from marriage out of a similar concern of hurting their father, they more typically fear surpassing him in career, and may feel guilty about excelling in a professional area where their dad was unsuccessful.

❏***The fear of increased responsibility.*** *Many worry also that success will bring greater responsibility into their life. This fear, of course, isn't without justification. Success usually does mean additional responsibility. While we may long for the benefits of reaching a goal, and the greater influence it will give us, we may fear that the additional challenge will tax us beyond our limits.*

We can also dread the increased sense of significance that will come with our achievement and the new responsibilities involved. We may fear that we're not up to handling it emotionally. Change in our self-concept is always unnerving--even positive change. We may feel squeamish or embarrassed about taking on responsibility that to us signals a boost in status.

❏**The fear of insignificance.** *At the same time we can be hampered by a rather different concern--that what we accomplish may be of no ultimate significance to human life anyway. Why bother to make the effort? So what if I slave to put myself through college and pull top grades as an economics major? So what if I land a good position with a corporation? What will I achieve that someone else couldn't accomplish just as well?*
What difference will it make if we have a second child? Billions of children have come into existence and died throughout history without making any impact on the world.

We are complex psychological creatures and often experience conflicting fears at the same time. One moment the thought of completing a goal unsettles us because we fear it will elevate us to more importance than we deserve. The next moment we're sapped by the thought that, even if we succeed, our achievement won't dent the world's problems.

Perspectives for Overcoming the Fear of Success
Since the anticipation of success can fill us with fears of both significance and insignificance, we need to learn to hold on to two perspectives at once. On the one hand, we should remind ourselves that Christ has a distinctive plan for our life. He has given us a combination of gifts and opportunities as unique from anyone else's as our fingerprints. The work we do may seem futile in a purely objective sense. Yes, we may take a job that could easily be filled by

39

someone else. Still, our personality and mix of gifts will allow us to relate to certain people for Christ within our work in ways no one else is as well-equipped to do. And, in the mystery of God's providence, we'll be there at just the right moment to meet certain needs of people that otherwise would go unheeded.

But a sense of futility can keep us from taking the steps so critical to keeping pace with his will. We must remind ourselves constantly that God's plan for us is personally designed so that the work we accomplish will contribute significantly to what Christ is doing to meet people's needs. God intends our life as a matchless gift to people. Others will be deprived of important benefits if we fail to act.

At the same time, we should remind ourselves that ultimately our work is only one small part of the picture of all that God is doing. We'll make plenty of mistakes, and the world won't expire as a result! Ultimately the work is God's, anyway, and we're forever in danger of taking ourselves too seriously.

In Overcoming the Fear of Success, psychologist Martha Friedman shares her own experience with the problem as a doctoral candidate and how she solved it:

"I was on the verge of becoming a Ph.D. dropout when a wise psychologist said to me, 'Why such a fuss? Nobody's going to read it anyway; it'll just gather dust on some college library shelf, and it'll certainly never be published. If you're meant to do important work, you'll do it after you get out of school.'

"I stopped obsessing, took a month off from my jobs, and finished my dissertation. While it's admittedly no major contribution to world science, it was a major contribution to my psyche. I had finished something important to me. It was . . . a matter of not magnifying what I was trying to accomplish."

*She adds," Minimizing the importance of a goal is an excellent way to reach that goal."**

We each need to work at achieving a healthy balance in the way we perceive our work. We need to know that what we do is significant; yet we must remember that we're instruments of a God who uses our weaknesses as effectively as our strengths. In Christ we can achieve this balance, for we can know that while our work is an important part of the help he extends to the world, he doesn't ultimately depend upon us but graciously uses our availability. With this knowledge, we can serve in a spirit of joyous victory, not defeat.

But What Will Others Think?
We also need to come to terms with our concern about how others may react to our success. The perception that others don't want us to succeed sometimes has basis. People don't always like it when we change. They may withdraw their affection. But we should remember that God has made us remarkably resilient as humans. We can bear the disappointment of lost affection if something positive takes its place. It can be a worthwhile tradeoff to let go of some affirmation in order to experience the joy of using our gifts more fully. And as we take steps of growth, we best position ourselves to develop new friendships.

In the long run we're happier in relationships with those who desire God's best for us, than with those who insist we conform to their still-life pictures.

Practical Steps
There are also some important practical steps we can take to manage our anxieties about success.

❏*The role of prayer. It is hard to exaggerate the importance of our personal devotional time as a setting for confronting our fears. We will benefit greatly by giving some generous attention during this time to quiet reflection. We need to dwell on God's grace and provision for our life, as well as stare our irrational fears in the face and recognize them for the straw men that they are. Make it a practice during your quiet time to prayerfully examine your fears of success and acknowledge their unreasonable nature. Remind yourself that God has put you on earth to be productive; he intends your life to be a gift to others. You are not fighting him by moving toward your goals, but cooperating with him, when these goals are ones he wants you to pursue.*

We should also make a point of establishing our priorities and daily schedule during our devotional time. When I've resolved in prayer that I should spend my time in certain ways during the day, I'm able to go forth with the confidence that I'm following God's intentions and not just my own impulses. The conviction of God's call, more than any factor, strengthens our motivation and quells our fears of both failure and success.

❑**Help from our friends.** *God's healing from our fears so often comes, in part, through the encouragement of friends, counselors, and those in our fellowship groups. What makes the fear of success so unsettling for many is the mistaken perception that they alone suffer from it. It's therapeutic simply to find just how universal the problem actually is. Seek relationships and, if possible, a support group, where you can be straightforward in sharing your apprehensions of success. You'll undoubtedly be relieved to find that others have the same concerns. Pray for each other and encourage one another as you move forward. The renewed confidence that comes from this interaction can be tremendous.*

If your fears of success have their roots in childhood traumas or a difficult upbringing, I would encourage you also to seek the help of a trained counselor. Take advantage of all the help you can get and, especially, of the best help available.

❑**Manage the benefits of success.** *Martha Friedman recommends that those who experience success shouldn't try to appropriate its benefits all at once. It takes time for our psyche to adapt to change, even welcome change. We need to be realistic about our own adjustment process and not make sudden drastic changes. If I'm granted a large salary increase, for instance, running out and buying a larger home may not be my wisest move. I may be happier simply making some improvements in my present one.*

As Christians we're well-schooled in the importance of not indulging ourselves with our

43

material benefits but using them to help others in need. Friedman's point adds a further incentive for keeping our lifestyle within reasonable bounds. Doing so makes good sense not only in view of our responsibility to the world but psychologically. Not that it's wrong for us as Christians to enjoy the benefits of success. Scripture extols the value of rejoicing in our achievements and enjoying the results of what we accomplish. The point is simply that balance is needed. We should remember, too, that if happiness is our goal, God has created us to find our greatest joy not in hoarding resources but in sharing them.

❏**Keep the wheels in motion.** Someone once asked Albert Einstein how he was able to cope with his great fame. He replied that he did so by continuing to work and pursue new goals. He didn't dwell on his successes but kept his mind actively involved with new challenges. His example speaks to the importance of keeping momentum in our life.

Give your attention to using the gifts Christ has given you, and to moving toward goals he helps you establish. We most fully experience Christ's motivation, and his healing of our fears, when our lives are in motion--not frantic, obsessive motion, but prudent, natural motion toward goals we've prayerfully resolved he wants us to pursue. It's through this moving forward in faith that we gain the "extra edge," to transcend our fears, and to find the courage to be whom Christ has made us to be. And we discover most completely and convincingly the truth of the biblical promise, that in his joy is our strength (Neh 8:10).
 (end)

Declaration

Father in Heaven, I declare that I am not afraid to arise to do all that You have called me to do, and to shine in the demonstration of your excellent Spirit upon me[23]. I am not afraid to let my light shine before men so that they can see the good works I do which glorify You.[24] I refuse to embrace a false sense of humility which causes me not to complete the work that You have purposed for me. I am ready to accept the responsibilities of the good success that You have in store for me. I depend on You totally, knowing that when I make mistakes, that You are a God of love and mercy and Your grace abounds for me. I thank You Father that I can move forward knowing that Your Holy Spirit is ever present to teach and guide me. I arise, for Your light has come and Your glory has risen upon me. I declare this to be a truth for my life in the name of Jesus. Amen.

---

[23] Isaiah 60:1
[24] Matthew 5:16

Fear – The Past Repeating Itself

2 Corinthians 5:17 - Therefore, if any man be in Christ, he is a new creature; old things are passed away; behold, all things are become new

There are some of us who find ourselves locked in a cycle of hurt. It has become so common place in our lives that we can almost predict the moment that we are going to experience hurt and rejection.

The hurt becomes an expectation. We almost look forward to it. Not only that, even if we do not see the likelihood of a recurrence of this hurtful event, we use the past to determine our expectation of the person we are with. We come to the stage where we say "all men are..," or "all women are...' Our past keeps determining our future.

As a matter of fact, we have a tendency to speak our expectations over our lives.

Such is the power given to us, by just being made in the image and likeness of God, that what we speak comes to pass. It is manifested in our lives daily. I wrote an article relating to this very subject on my blog last year.

When Old Injuries Come Back

I used to have this neck injury. As usual I was peacefully minding my own business, sitting in my friend's car when a taxi driver nearly caused him to have an accident. The front wheel on the passenger side dropped into a small hole and I felt my neck move to the side and back. I thought nothing of it until about three days later when I woke up in extreme pain. I could not move my neck or my back. I went to the doctor and was given anti-inflammatory medicine. When I went to get the x-ray the doctor told me that based on the movement of my neck, it could have been broken. I suffered for weeks with this thing until it finally subsided. I noticed however, that when I was under extreme stress, I would experience this pain. It was so bad that I would not be able to move my back at all and had to seek the help of a chiropractor.

I do not know when the light bulb went on in my head that when I was under stress I actually EXPECTED to experience this pain.... and naturally I did. I decided that I was under this burden long enough and when I noticed that I was under stress, I decided to get above it. I refused to let stress get the better of me. I refused to accept pain and suffering. In a short

47

time, I realized that I was not experiencing this pain anymore and that has been years now.

In the same way, remembering the things that others do to hurt us cause us an immense amount of pain. These old injuries have a way of resurfacing even though we say we have forgiven. My Pastor puts it this way "when we forgive someone, we "dis-member" the hurt. However when we "re-member" the hurt we are actually retrieving it from where it was cast and putting it back together." Have you ever tried to put together a jig saw puzzle? Remembering a past offense is like doing just that. My friend Judene once said "God cast her sins in the sea of forgetfulness and He has put a NO FISHING sign there". If you keep remembering past offenses, you are fishing illegally. In other words, you have control over what you will allow into your space. You can choose what to remember. If something triggers this memory, you can refuse to entertain the thought. Every sin including unforgiveness begins with a thought.

Your body, mind (soul) and spirit are what makes up your temple. Just as the physical temple has gates and walls, you have gates and walls around your temple. Your gates are your praise and your walls – your salvation (Isaiah 60:18). Praise is our gateway to God. For indeed as we are saved from our enemies our deliverance becomes a wall around us – a stronghold against the enemy and our praise become our gates (Excerpt from AND THE PRISONERS HEARD THEM [S Dallas]).

A wound cannot get better if you keep picking at it. It is more likely to become infected, poisoning the system and aggravating the injury. Everything the enemy throws at us is designed for one of three things – to steal, to kill or to destroy. Someone once said that unforgiveness is like drinking poison and expecting the other person to die. It just does not work that way. I guarantee that it will steal your joy, destroy your friendship and cause death to your purpose.

Do you really want the burdens of unforgiveness, resentment and bitterness? Cast your cares upon Jesus for He cares for you (1 Peter 5:7) He also said that we are to give Him our burdens for His yoke is easy and His burden is light (Matthew 11:30).Now that is an offer you should not refuse.
Excerpt from The Better Direction[2]

When my previous marriage ended, I was deeply hurt. Two years later, I was speaking to my cousin Roxy, relating to him the circumstances of the breakup. He said to me "you are still hurting." My response was in the affirmative. He then said something to me that I have tried to remember every time I am tempted to dwell on the past. "When you are driving, occasionally you need to glance in the rear view mirror to see what is behind you. But you have to keep your attention

---

[2] http://sylviadallas.com

focused in front of you in order to avoid the crash and burn." Very sage words indeed.

I thought I could not find any advice to better this until I read Paul's letter to the Philippians - **Brethren, I do not regard myself as having laid hold of it yet; but one thing I do: forgetting what lies behind and reaching forward to what lies ahead,14I press on toward the goal for the prize of the upward call of God in Christ Jesus.**[25] Please note that Paul urges us to **forget what lies behind. WHAT A REVOLUTIONARY IDEA!!** I do not even need to see what is behind me.

It is unfair to your prospective spouse, to judge them according to the hurt that was inflicted upon you by another person. Would you like such a burden to carry? I think not. We cannot forget a hurt if we are not willing to forgive. Our forgiveness towards each other is not based on whether or not the person to whom we must extend this mercy is repentant. As Christians, we are called

---

[25] Phillipians 3:13-14

to forgive them anyway. A common statement heard when the subject of forgiveness is mentioned is "Well I will forgive, but I won't forget" - Why? Why would you want to keep remembering an hurt? What possible benefit can it bring to you? When you are tempted to put back together the jigsaw puzzle of the past hurts you have "dismembered", ask yourself if you really want to make that investment of time and energy. Did not the Lord say to us that He "blots out our transgressions, remembering them no more"[26]? He expects us to do the same.

Declaration

My Father, thank You that you have forgiven all my sins, even before I have committed them. I declare my ears closed to the voice of the enemy. Thank You that you have blotted out my past and remember it no more. I know that by the Spirit of Adoption, I can call you Abba. I am a new creation in Christ because I accepted Him as Lord and Saviour of my life. I declare that my spouse is not cut from the same cloth as

---

[26] Isaiah 43:25

those who have hurt me. Instead I thank you that he/she has my best interests at heart and just as You blot out my transgressions and remember them no more, I know you have done the same for them. I am doing what Your apostle Paul said - I forget which lies behind and look forward to the goal for the prize of Your call upon my life.

I declare this to be a truth for my life in the name of Jesus. Amen.

Fear - Abandonment

Abandonment - to leave completely and finally: forsake utterly, desert. To give up, discontinue, withdraw from[27].

I was in the first edit stage of this book when I realized that there was an entire section that was not written. I tried for several days to write this section but could get nowhere. I was at the point of throwing in the towel. Every time I sat down to write, I would freeze, or distract myself with something else.

---

[27] Http://dictionary.com

I have always thought of myself as a fairly emotionally secure person. Why was it so difficult for me to write this section? I almost deleted the section and declare the book finished, but the Holy Spirit kept prompting me. A good friend told me that confronting a fear is the only way to make it go away.

Thoughts of my father's death came to me (he died when I was three years old). I reasoned that there was no way I could have thought he abandoned me, he died. He had no control over that and furthermore he was 70 years old when he died. Shortly thereafter, my mother sent my sister and I to live in the country with my grand aunt and uncle. It was not the most pleasant time for me. Even then I knew that if my mother had a choice, there was no way that she would separate us. Somehow there was a root of abandonment issues that I needed to get to the bottom of. I had to examine this from my perspective, and my experiences. While my life is an open book (especially after this publication), that does not extend to the rest of my family. I am not at liberty to speak of their experiences.

I realize based on my experience that persons with abandonment issues tend to be the first to end a relationship. It's a case of seeing the hurt coming, knowing that there is nothing you can do to avoid it, so you run. When it comes to running from hurt, Usain Bolt has nothing on me. I used to say all the time "I run away from what hurts me." When you do not confront the things that you fear, they find a way of coming back like a recurring decimal in your life.

I was in a relationship once, where I was in such a rage most of the time, I would jump in my vehicle in the wee hours of the morning, drive to Montego Bay at the fastest possible speed and get back home before daybreak. Just to vent my anger. Now that I can look objectively at the situation, that was downright suicidal and monumentally stupid.

The fear of abandonment has been described as a self-sabotaging phobia. It causes behaviour that brings about the thing that you fear. Job said during his trials, that the thing he feared most had come upon him. Some of the persons who experience this fear (like I did), tend to become outwardly extremely independent, but privately are needy. This outward and fiercely demonstrated independence is our wall of defense. We try to refrain from getting close to people so that they do not see this vulnerable side of us. On the rare occasion that we allow someone into our space, we are sure to have our defense mechanisms well-tuned and ready.

Betrayal in any form hurts, but betrayal through abandonment is probably the most gut wrenching of all. When trust is abused, that is a form of abandonment. The issue of trust is very important in a relationship. Any relationship not built on trust is in trouble from the very start. When you commit to getting married, you are making a declaration of trust to your spouse. You are saying I trust you with my life, I trust you with my emotions, I trust you to love me, I trust you to be truthful, I trust you. The minute that trust is broken by a lie (of any kind), the pain is immeasurable.

I remember telling Rohan that when you trust someone and you both agree to tell the truth to each other, it is like getting a shiny new penny and you treasure it because you know that no one else has a penny that shiny. When you are caught in a lie, the penny becomes dull and begins to look common.

Why do we lie? Is it that we believe the person's expectations of us are unrealistic and therefore we prefer to lie our way through? Have our spouses ever made us feel unsafe to tell the truth? I had to ask myself the very uncomfortable question, "What makes my husband feel unsafe to tell me the truth about his smoking?"

I asked the Holy Spirit, "why do people lie?" He responded by asking me why I do not lie. My only answer was this "prior to coming into a knowledge of You living in me, I did not lie because I was too lazy to try to remember the lie(s) I would have to tell to back up the first lie, so the easiest method was not to lie. That is not to say a few did not escape from me. Now that I know You live in me I just don't want to offend / grieve You." He then pressed me again "Are you afraid to tell the truth?" I responded in the negative. He said "a lot of people lie because they are listening to a voice that tells them it is unsafe to tell the truth"

Well blow me down with a feather!!!

The Holy Spirit also revealed to me that when there is a situation where one person in the relationship is a new believer, they are afraid to slip up because they fear the judgment of the more mature believer. I cried. Was I communicating to Rohan that I would judge him, quarrel with him if he was smoking again, when all I really wanted to do was to point him to help? I asked the Lord to give me an opportunity to show him that I had not abandoned him in this way. The Holy Spirit ministered to me in this area also. He pointed out to me that being unequally yoked is not just about being saved and unsaved. It also refers to levels of maturity. When the level of maturity between two Christians is vastly different, the less mature person, when they slip up is fearful of being judged by the more mature Christian.

I remember an occasion before we got married, that I almost cheated on Rohan.

I realized the situation that I had gotten myself into and before I could cross the boundary, I ran home to him. I was smiling and laughing as if nothing happened, but he called me out. "What's wrong?" he asked me. I asked him what he meant and he said "the sun is not shining" – meaning that my smile was not reaching my eyes. I asked myself at that time "truth or lie?" I decided to tell him the truth.

Me: "I almost cheated on you"

Him: "Did you?"

Me: "No I did not, I tucked my tail between my legs and came home as fast as I could"

Him: "What are you still searching for that you felt that you had to look elsewhere?"

We spoke for nearly half the night. I honestly do not remember what was said, but when we were finished, I felt safe.

Abandonment leaves a void that feels very much like an abyss. It just never seems to have an end. It causes the person who experiences it to turn inward on themselves. They ask themselves what is wrong with them why the person left. They become their own torturer, constantly analyzing and reasoning. Even though the reasons for the person leaving them may have nothing to do with them but issues that the person is going through, they keep asking, "was there anything I did to drive them away?" "Was there something about me that needed to change?" I went through my fair share of it, until my defense mechanism kicked in and I made sure that I was the person who left.

I began to live by a code of running from anything that hurts me. While I was writing this book, Rohan and I had a major quarrel. As a matter of fact, for the duration of the process of writing this book, my marriage felt like a spiritual war zone. But with regard to this particular incident, some very hurtful things were said to me. I will not go into the details, but suffice it to say, that when he was finished, I was sure that he was definitely going to abandon me and our marriage, and my flight response had kicked in. The next day, I had to go to Negril to visit my aunt. I had decided that I was not returning but as Ezekiel said, "the hand of the Lord was strong upon me" and I returned home "in the heat of my spirit."

I kept crying and asking Him why I should return home to a man who does not appreciate me. His response was that I needed to face my challenges, my fears in order to conquer them. I remember telling Him that I have been dealing with this fear for so long that it was beginning to feel like the only faithful companion I had. I think that was the first time I ever admitted to having a fear of being abandoned. The Lord reminded me that He would never leave me, nor has He ever. He reminded me that He never gave me a spirit of fear and that I must resist all things from the devil.

In the name of Jesus, I refuse to accept any fear as my constant companion and declare that the Holy Spirit is my true companion, teacher and comforter. Amen.

I have been having some really serious encounters with the Lord during this time as the Holy Spirit ministered to me. One thing I have learned from this, no matter how far and how fast you feel you can run from a situation or circumstance, at some point you have to stop and face it.

What now? Facing the fear does not guarantee that Rohan will not abandon me, but if that were to happen, I now know that it will not destroy me. The way forward is putting my trust in God to repair this marriage. I am prepared to trust Him with everything concerning this marriage. I have His promises that (a) He will never leave me nor forsake me, (b) that He who has started a good work is faithful to bring it to completion, and (c) He will perfect all things concerning me.

Declaration

My Father, never again will I believe that I am abandoned. I believe Your promise that You will never leave or forsake me. I believe Your promise, that You will be with me to the end of this age. I believe that Your Holy Spirit is with me at all times to guide and teach me. I say like David, though my mother, father, friends, family, even my church may forsake me, You will take me up.[28] I AM NOT ALONE. I declare this to be a truth for my life in the name of Jesus. Amen.

---

[28] PSALM 27:10

The Misplacement Of Our Faith

I really could not close out this section on fear unless I covered the issue of faith and the things or persons we place our faith in.

Hebrews 11:1-6 gives us a clear definition of faith. It is the *substance of things hoped for, the evidence of things not seen.* Without it, *it is impossible to please God.*

When we place our faith in anything or in a person, we become totally dependent on that thing or person not letting us down. I made the mistake of placing my faith in Rohan and in our marriage. I believe that somewhere in the deep recesses of my heart, I believed that he would never let me down, but he has – several times. I am sure also, that in his perception, I have let him down also. Indeed he and my marriage have been proven to be very fallible.

According to The Free Dictionary (thefreedictionary.com), misplacement is *the act of losing something.* To misplace is *to put in a wrong place, to mislay, to bestow confidence on an improper, unsuitable, idea or person.*

Do not think that I am advocating a lack of trust in marriage. I am simply saying that when our faith is in the correct place, it is less likely for us to be destroyed by betrayal of any kind. All of us are fallible and are likely to hurt each other at some point in our lives despite our best intentions.

To say we have lost faith in someone or something is to declare that we really have misplaced our faith. Let's say that you want to fill a glass with water, would you not place it under the tap or the bottle from which the water will come? If you had placed the empty glass anywhere else but under the source of the water, would you say that you were let down by the source or that you had misplaced the glass? We become disappointed in God when we misplace our faith, when we become afraid that He will not come through for us – especially in the way we expect, when we have a view of the outcome that is not in accordance to His will and timing, when we place our faith in **our** understanding of what should happen.

Fear is a destroyer of faith. Fear causes us to always ask "what if?" I remember my earlier days after my recommitment to the Lord, I would always ask my Pastor "what if...?" His response would always be "what if your nose was a door post?" The "what if" questions are designed to plant doubts in our minds, when what God wants is for us to trust Him completely.

Has there ever been a time when He was not faithful? Has He ever broken His Word? Has He ever lied? He has promised us that heaven and earth will pass away before His Word fails. His promises are always, "Yea" and "Amen". If the answers to these questions are all no, then it is time we put our faith in its rightful place – in God.

Placing your faith in God does not mean that we will not face disappointment when we see our spouses not living up to the potential of their purpose. It means though, that with our faith in its rightful place, we know we can trust God to cause His Holy Spirit to move upon the hearts of our spouses, thereby positioning them to fulfill their purposes. It means that we pray towards this expected end with hope in our hearts, that God's ultimate purpose for our spouses will be fulfilled. It means that we do not embrace disappointment and depression when we do not see it coming to pass in the time we expect. It means complete and total trust in God. Disappointment requires an emotional investment of energy that exhausts and depletes us. God wants us to rest in Him and depend on Him. Every time that I feel frustrated about where Rohan is in his walk with Christ, I remember that though I was saved at 10 years old, I spent 36 years in the wilderness before coming to the realization of who I am in Christ and into relationship with Him. I pray that it will not take that long for him, and even though I experience my bouts of anxiety in this regard, I am still trusting God to take him where he needs to be.

Faith – the substance of my hope for him and the evidence of what I know to be true but have not yet seen.

Chapter Four: What Is Defilement?

Defilement - *The act of making defiled.*
Defiled - *to make foul, dirty, unclean, pollute, debase.*

Marriage should be honored by all, and the marriage bed undefiled, For God will judge the adulterer and all the sexually immoral. - Hebrews 13:4

The word undefiled is represented by the Greek word amiantos[29] which means literally "unsoiled or pure". We see in the latter part of the verse that God will judge the adulterer (the person causing the defilement)

What are the ways in which our marriage bed can be defiled? In Leviticus we see a virtual laundry list of ways in which we can defile ourselves.

1 Corinthians 6:18 tells us to *"flee fornication. Every sin that a man doeth*

---

[29] *Strong's G283)*

is without the body; but he that commiteth fornication sinneth against his own body".

Consider this. Would you walk into church and drop/hike your garments and defecate in the corner. Considering that our bodies are the temple of the living God, is that not what we are doing when we commit fornication, soiling the temple? Joseph asked in Genesis 39:9 "how then can I do this wicked thing and sin against God[30]?" Yes - fornication is a wicked thing.

We often rationalise our actions. "I am getting married to this person anyway." "It is ok, we both attend the same church and we plan to get married." Or the most widely used "God understands." NO! NO! NO! Nowhere in the Bible is permission given to us to live a life of sin. As a matter of fact we are called to be holy as He (God) is holy[31]

Have you ever had an abortion? Or gave permission for one? How long have you kept this secret sin hidden in your heart?

---

[30] Genesis 39:9
31 Leviticus 20:26 & 1 Peter 1:16

The burden of hiding a secret sin slowly kills you inside and affects your purpose, your marriage, your great ideas, everything about your life. Fornication does the same thing in principle. The act itself looses a spirit of lust and depravity in your life. The lack of self-control leads to a constant desire to satisfy the fleshly desires and develops into uncontrolled appetites.

Another form of defilement as sexual sin is pornography. As a child at the age of ten, I was introduced to sex via pornography. I became addicted to it. I was conscious of feeling dirty every time that I participated, but kept being strangely drawn to it. I never understood what was happening to me until I was in my forties. I struggled with this thing for years, suffering in silence, but putting on a brave front. I did not know where to turn for help. I found that someone with my vivid imagination eventually got bored with the regular fare and started to seek out more "interesting" stories. I got tired of watching porn. I began to search for websites that had "good literature" on the subject. Yet a deep part of me realized that I was sinking into a miry pit.

When I met my husband, he told me quite frankly, that the only shows he liked to watch were animal shows (like Wild Discovery and National Geographic) and sex shows. By this time, I was making quite a name for myself as a photographer and getting famous for photographing nudes). I rationalised that I was simply photographing the beauty of the physical body - a very Grecian mindset. I was also known in the field of poetry as a sensuous poet. I started to wean myself from porn movies and erotic literature. I asked my husband (we were not married at the time) not to bring any porn movies to the house. After I explained myself, he agreed.

The cleaning up of my life began in earnest in 2007, with my recommitment to God. The damage was already done. I had consumed so much filth over the years that I was polluted in my thoughts especially. I think that apart from God keeping me all those years, what saved me was the fact that I had a boundary that I was determined not to cross, but I was coming dangerously close - skirting the edge - if you will. Could I really be saved? I was not questioning my salvation experience. I was asking myself, if I was beyond repair? I saw myself as damaged goods. I reminded myself over and over until I was convinced, that I served a God to whom NOTHING is impossible, and that He is the God to whom EVERYTHING is possible.

If you have been divorced as we both were, then there is the issue of covenant breaking to deal with. That in addition to all the others is a recipe for trouble.

Rohan and I planned to get married on July 22, 2011 and decided to abstain for one month (which he eventually pared down to 2 weeks) prior to our wedding.

Chapter Five: Abstaining - Sweeter Honeymoon or Period of Sanctification?

Often couples that have lived together, once they decide to get married, choose (more often than not) to abstain from sex for a short period before they get married. The reason is often to "make the honeymoon sweeter". It is really represents a conscious decision which declares "let us sin (fornicate) up to this time and then wait until marriage."

The honeymoon should be a time of bonding, of unfolding and discovering the mysteries of each other. Unfortunately that is already negated by the fact that we have lived together outside the sanctity of marriage and there is really no mystery to unfold. Consider this. Is it that we are planning to do the act of sex differently during the honeymoon?

In reality, all we end up doing is simply feed a craving, or slake a thirst. It feels good after being apart even though we were craving each other, but after that, what's next? It really has become an issue of lust more than anything else.

Sex as it is supposed to be in the context of marriage and is about two people **discovering** each other in a deeply intimate way. The definition of *discover* according to dictionary.com is *to see, to gain knowledge of, learn of, find or find out, gain sight or knowledge of (something previously unseen or unknown)*. In biblical times, when a man and woman engaged in sexual intercourse, it was said that they knew each other. The first such mention is Genesis 4:1 – *Adam knew Eve.* This knowing usually led to pregnancy and subsequent births. It is the time of two becoming one. It is an act of worship. Why do I say that the sexual act is an act of worship? The word used in Genesis 4:1 is actually "yada – pronounced yaw-dah [Strong's 3045]". To speak of knowing someone is to declare that your can perceive, understand, experience that person. The word Yada(h) is actually a type of worship – in which one gives over oneself in worship in adoration. (Sounds familiar?) Therefore I will posit this question to you my dear reader – *When you were fornicating, which altar were you worshipping at? Or what were you giving worship to?*

In 1 Corinthians 6:16, it notes that those who fornicate with a harlot becomes one with her. It therefore stands to reason, that when a married couple have sex, they have become one. Two single entities have left their mothers and fathers and now cleave to each other.

Is there a difference between desire and lust? I believe so.

Lust (dictionary.com) *Intense sexual desire or appetite. Uncontrolled or illicit sexual desire or appetite; lecherousness*

Desire: *To wish or long for; crave, want. To express a wish to obtain; ask for*

I would rather be the desire of my husband's heart for intimacy with me than the object of his lust. His lust can be satisfied by anyone. His desire is

74

satisfied by me. Lust is a poor imitation of intimacy. It only satisfies the physical but leaves the spirit starving.

The period of abstention therefore should be about consecrating our lives afresh before God. When we are taking part in the marriage ceremony, we have come before the altar of the Lord. In the scriptures we see time and time again, where the people of God went through a period of consecration before coming before the altar of the Lord. It is not different for us. Instead of being washed ritualistically in water, that area of our lives is now brought under the cleansing and sanctifying Blood of Jesus. In addition, because of Grace, we can approach the Throne boldly, confess our sin and receive mercy.

Let us not fool ourselves. Living in a state of fornication are really self-control and disobedience issues.

Self-control is one of the fruits of the Spirit that we should have acquired **prior** to marriage. If we could not control our urges before marriage, are we likely to be able to do so after marriage? Remember, that period of singleness really was supposed to teach us self-control.

Disobedience is as witchcraft before God, and I believe willful disobedience - even more so. Willful disobedience causes the anointing to depart from us. In 1 Samuel 15, we see where willful disobedience caused the Spirit of the Lord to depart from Saul. When you subject yourself to a different kind of spirit instead of the Spirit of The Lord, the anointing departs from your life. Once again, happily the Lord is willing to take us back with joy, once we confess our sins and repent.

If your house is dirty, does it become clean just because you have put up new drapes? What about your bed? Is it clean if you spread a clean sheet on top of a dirty one? The principle is that the house must be swept, or the sheets on the bed must be changed. We are speaking here of sanctification. How do we go about becoming sanctified?

The Sanctification Process

What does it mean to be sanctified? It means to set part or declare as holy. Does this mean that you go through a ritual? Certainly not! The real deal for us Christians is that we are sanctified by the Blood of Jesus. When we come before God with confession, a sincere heart for repentance and accept his forgiveness by faith, we become sanctified. Acts 20:32 *And now, brethren, I commend you to God, and to the word of His Grace, which is able to build you up, and to give you an inheritance among all them which are sanctified.*

Romans 3:13 *For if you live according to the flesh, you will die; but if by the Spirit you put to death the deeds of the body you will live.*

The truth is that no matter how we try to rationalize it, sex before marriage is wrong. It does not matter if you will soon be married to this person, sex is really for the person that you **are married to**. Fornication really demonstrates a lack of self-control - one of the fruits of the

Spirit. Research actually shows that persons who have sex before marriage are more likely to cheat on their spouses during marriage. Acts 20:32 tells us that the *"word of His Grace"* is *"able to build us up"*

What does this mean for us? By accepting that our sins have been forgiven, we pave the way to move more easily into the things of God. When we are tortured by our past, it keeps us from moving towards our future. There are a lot of things in our past that we find it difficult to forgive ourselves for. If God Himself has forgiven our sins, are we saying that it is not enough? Such an attitude is living under condemnation, which is of the devil.

The Holy Spirit will bring something to your attention not to condemn you but to convict you. There is a big difference. Condemnation says "you will never get it right". Conviction says "this has gone wrong, here is how it can be fixed".

Now therefore, there is now no condemnation for them that are in Christ

Jesus[32]. This means that once we recognize that we have strayed off the path, our sole focus must be quickly accessing the forgiveness and mercy that has already been extended to us by way of the cross by confession and repentance, and get back on the path. No self-flagellation is necessary here. Condemnation is not for those who abide in Christ, so do not receive it.

This book is not meant for anyone to live under condemnation. Jesus shed His Blood so that we can approach the throne of grace boldly, not in presumption, not in contempt, but assured of His love and mercy towards us. We can climb into our Father's lap and confess our sin and say "Daddy, I did this thing and I am truly sorry". His Word says, *If we confess our sins He is just to forgive us and cleanse us of all unrighteousness".*[33] We do not have to wait for a period before the forgiveness "kicks in", we are forgiven immediately. If, as Christians, we keep excavating the

---

[32] Romans 8:1

[33] 1 John 1:9

"old man" and returning to our sinful ways, we give the enemy an accusation against us.

There is a difference between "godly sorrow" and "worldly sorrow". The first, "godly sorrow" says, "I will never return to this", and all actions thereafter demonstrates this. "Worldly sorrow" says " I am sorry that I got caught" and you never really see any change. Our objective should always be to turn away from the things we do that are wrong.

Chapter Six: Understanding Covenants

What is a covenant? According to dictionary.com it is a noun which means *"an agreement, usually formal, between two or more persons to do or not to do something specified."*

The Hebrew word *Berit* means agreement between two parties

Covenant is a solemn, binding arrangement between two parties and entails a variety of responsibilities, benefits and penalties depending on the specific covenant. It is usually accompanied by signs (witnesses, memorials, shared meals), solemn binding oaths - sealing the relationship with promises of blessing for keeping the covenant and curses for breaking the covenant. Sometimes it involves a written document on which the words of the covenant, its terms in the form of promises and stipulations are spelled out, witnessed to, signed and sealed.

When we enter into marriage, we enter into a covenant relationship with each other similar to the relationship that Jesus has with His Bride - The Church. Husbands are to love their wives as Christ loves the church and wives are to submit to their husbands. The sexual act is what seals the covenant.

The first thing that sparks fear in most women (especially today's women who are independent and very much in charge of their lives) is the submission part. I was so afraid of that word that I refused to say the word "obey" in the vows during my first wedding. The pastor repeated the vows, probably thinking that I did not hear him the first time. So that part of the ceremony sounded like this:

Pastor: Please repeat after me, I Sylvia Straw do promise to love, honor and obey...

Me: I, Sylvia Straw, do promise to love and honor...

Pastor: I, Sylvia Straw, do promise to love, honor and obey...

Me: I, Sylvia Straw, do promise to love and honor...

At which point I turned to the beleaguered groom and informed him that we can just live together. He instructed the pastor to move on with the ceremony.

To some people the preceding information might seem funny. I certainly thought so at the time when I would retell the story, but hindsight is 20/20 vision. It is important to note that we never went for pre-marital counseling. Rohan told me that he never went either and we both decided to do it differently this time around.

Looking back, I realize that my former husband must have felt betrayed by my position. Even if he did not, (perhaps he did not understand the significance of that action) I certainly recognize now that I had set the stage for rebellion, betrayal and judgment in my marriage and 7 years later, it was over. In my former marriage, I kept my maiden name as a sign of my independence, but after coming into an understanding of submission and what it meant in the biblical context, as a symbol of my heart posture, I now use only Rohan's name - Dallas.

The word submission as used in the scriptures really means that wives must respect their husbands. Nowhere does it say we cannot disagree with him. A lot of men misuse that scripture as a means of subjecting their wives to tyranny. Yet, reading the scripture in its entirety indicates that there are stipulations for **both** parties on how each should be treated with consideration for the emotional well-being of each other.

Wives are often told – "submit to your husbands" and that is true. Often overlooked is the verse in 1 Peter3:7 that clearly states how a husband should treat his wife *so that nothing hinders your [his] prayers*.

Acts 5:1-11 tells us the story of Ananias and Sapphira. In a nutshell, they both agreed to sell a piece of property and lie that they had sold it for a lesser amount. The issue was not in the amount of money that was presented (as some people like to believe), but that they had lied to the Holy Spirit. I bring up this example to ask the question "Does being submitted to her husband mean that Sapphira had to walk in unrighteousness with her husband?" I believe that she could have respectfully disagreed with (submitting to) her husband on this course of action and since he had chosen to go along with it anyway, she could have confessed to Peter, "Look, the amount we sold it for was "x" dollars but we have decided to give this percentage of the money to the church." I do not see anywhere in the Bible where we are called to lie for each other – do you? We can joyfully debate this one in another forum.

Every aspect of our marriage is covered under the covenant that we made before God and man. The emotional, physical, financial and spiritual well-being of each person is governed by this covenant. Rohan and I have what would be considered a strange ritual. Each evening we see each other - after the usual greeting - the first question we ask each other is "do you have money?" Strange isn't it? But we have a reason for doing so. We are both self-employed. Our work, being seasonal in their peaks, means that at one time or another, one of us is without ready cash. Our peak periods do not always coincide. Therefore one of us might have money and the other does not. We share with each other all the time. I do not subscribe to the old adage that "what's mine is mine and what's his is mine".

Why ask? Why not just dole out money to each other? We recognize that based on the duties that we have unconsciously taken on, he or I might have something to pay for, and if the other person has funds, there is no need to touch money that does not need to be touched. It works for us.

In the same breath, the other aspects of our marriage need to be looked after. If I have an emotional concern that keeps coming up, he needs to reassure me and try to help me to get to the root of said concern until it is settled in my mind and vice versa. The issues of physical and spiritual also need to be addressed based on the covenant that we have made with each other. We are supposed to look out for each other's well-being.

Based on our vows, in promising to "love each other through sickness and health, for richer, for poorer, till death do us part", intrinsic to that promise is that we will do all that is possible to act responsibly with regards to our health. That includes healthy eating habits, eschewing addictive habits and seeking help where necessary. It means that for any part of our well-being (spiritual, emotional, physical and financial) that is not functioning as it should, we should seek help, so that those areas are functioning optimally at all times.

Everything about our marriage must be addressed in the context of "the covenant".

Let's keep it real, lest you think that I am saying that my marriage to Rohan is euphoric. Nothing could be further from the truth. We constantly butt heads especially in the areas of physical and spiritual well-being, and yes, we are both Christians.

There is no perfection here on earth, we are only perfected in Christ Jesus. A common misconception about salvation is that once saved, everything is going to be alright. Wrong! Upon salvation, we have been pulled out of darkness into His marvelous light. The attention of the enemy is now upon us. In the same way, choosing to get married instead of living together outside the sanctity of marriage, causes the spotlight to shine on you. The enemy is going to turn up his game. He is coming at you with devices, most of which will surprise you.

I have found that the state of a marriage is dependent on each party's relationship with God. Therefore, if the couple has a deepening relationship with God, their marriage is more harmonious. If one person, as I said earlier, believes that once they are saved there is not much else for them to do, they will carry that same attitude into their marriage. They will believe that once married, everything is alright. That can only be fixed by fervent prayer.

Covenant of Death

I had a vision once. I saw a couple in the courts of Heaven asking God to help their marriage. They were asking why they were having so much difficulty in their marriage and why it seems that their prayers were not answered. In a corner of the courtroom, the devil waved a sheet of paper and shouted "Still valid, still valid!!" On the paper was written "contract of death through fornication"

At the time Rohan and I were going through some difficulties in our marriage. The enemy really run riot in my mind. There were trust issues, impotence, quarrels, you name it we were going through it. It seemed as if we got over one hurdle only to have to jump another. There were tears and frustrations aplenty.

I was an uncommitted Christian living with Rohan at the time we decided to get married. He was not yet saved. By the time we went for our first counseling session, he accepted Jesus Christ as Lord and Saviour.

I told him about the dream and we both prayed for our marriage, confessing the sin of fornication and receiving the forgiveness of Jesus Christ. It was not smooth sailing immediately after but the challenges became easier to bear.

Colossians 2:14 speaks about the ordinances written against us. When we embrace a life of sin, we give the enemy opportunities to write accusations against us and stand accusing us. When we choose to sin, we embrace death. When we choose to obey God and follow His way we embrace life.

Covenant of Life

Colossians 2:14

And through the divine authority of His cross, He cancelled out every legal violation we had on our record and the old arrest warrant that stood to indict us. He erased all - our sins, our stained soul, and our shameful failure to keep His laws - He deleted it all and they cannot be retrieved! Everything we once were in Adam has been placed onto His cross and nailed there permanently as a public display of cancellation (TPT)

Hebrews 12:24

You have come to Jesus, the one who mediates the new covenant between God and people, and to the sprinkled blood, which speaks of forgiveness, instead of crying out for vengeance like the blood of Abel (NLT)

Hebrews 9:15

That is why He is the one who mediates a new covenant between God and people so that all who are call can receive the eternal inheritance God has promised them. For Christ died to set them free from the penalty of the sins they had committed under that first covenant. (NLT)

In the days of the Roman Empire, when someone was being adopted, in front of seven witnesses, the judge would take the old birth certificate and wipe off all the writing. He would then re-write the person new adoption information on the paper. The person being adopted could not be accused or tried in court for any crime committed up to that time because that person no longer existed. A new person would walk out of that courtroom.

The Spirit that we received has brought us by adoption into sonship so that we can cry out "Abba Father."[Romans 8:15]

Therefore the enemy cannot rightfully accuse us of what we used to do before we got saved.

We are no longer under a covenant of death through Adam but rather a covenant of life through the death, burial and resurrection of Jesus Christ. This was God's gift to us - one of His Divine

Grace which embodies His justness, His love, His mercies.

What happens when as Christians we choose to walk in a sinful life? Do we say, "I have Grace so I am forgiven already?" Do we continue in sin so that Grace will abound?[Romans 6:1] Grace actually enables and empowers us to resist sin. Paul in Romans 6:1 says *"Certainly not!"* Again, what if we do sin? Do we beat upon ourselves? Rent our garments and sit in ashes for an appropriate time? Surely the Holy Spirit will be displeased and keep reminding us over and over of our sin!

No brethren! If you feel such condemnation, then I assure you that it is not the Holy Spirit in action. He will convict you that you have sinned, but He also leads you to the way of repentance. Remember, conviction says "this has gone wrong, but here is the way to correct that", while condemnation says "you have done this wrong, it is your fault, you are going to be punished until you get it right, and you will never get it right so it will always be on your conscience".

Establishing The New Covenant

Throughout the history of the Bible, when the Israelites went into a new territory, their first order of business was always to tear down the altars of Baal and erect altars to God.

God Himself tells us He is a jealous God. The altars of our idols cannot exist in the Presence of God. A striking example of this is seen when the Phillistines had the effrontery to place the captured Ark of the Presence of the Lord beside their God Dagon which the Lord destroyed.[1 Samuel 5:2-5]

We have to remove the idols in our lives because they cannot exist in the Presence of God. If it means that we must re-commit our lives to the Lord, then let us do so. Let us declare over our marriages what the Word of God says. When we speak out loud our intentions, as we did when we made our vows, we are bringing into action and existence that which we have declared.

In natural law, an old covenant (contract) has to be cancelled or made invalid before commitment to a new contract. This old contract is terminated by (a) violation of the contract terms (b) buying out the contract. The old contract was purchased with the Blood of Jesus, so just like the Roman adoption process, the enemy has nothing on you anymore because the old you does not exist anymore. But what if after our salvation, we consciously and deliberately choose to continue sinning, in this case fornicating? We would have now moved into the area of willfully sinning. The enemy, as in the vision, now has an accusation against you, because by willfully choosing to continue in a life of sin, you have come back into covenant with him.

I was just reading a post on the internet about actress Jamie Lee Curtis being married for 31 years. This is an astounding feat in the atmosphere of short lived marriages in Hollywood. When asked about the secret of longevity of her marriage, her response was "Do Not Divorce".

There is no easy street in marriage, or as a Christian for that matter. I see nowhere in the Bible that we will have an easier time. The promise that I do see is that He will never leave us nor forsake us and that He will be with us even to the end of time. His Presence is what makes the difficulties easier to bear and enables us to triumph over the devices of the enemy. It is what enables us to be faithful to this new covenant in our lives.

Can an old and new covenant co-exist? Can you imagine that I have a contract with you to provide some services to you for "x" price. You happen to meet someone who is offering a far superior service for a much better price. Do I have a right to take you to court if you do not terminate my contract before you take up the other? The two contracts cannot co-exit. One has to be cancelled.

God is a God of order and He operates in the legal framework of His Word. I spoke to a friend of mine who is a lawyer. One of the things that she told me is that in the natural when a prisoner pleads guilty in the court of law, he must benefit in some way from his confession. This usually comes in the form of a reduced sentence. The benefit that I consider really special and of great importance to Christians, is that once confession takes place, the court accepts our version of the events and not the accuser's version. For us also, our sentence is not reduced, it is repealed. Hallelujah!!!

The Importance Of Confession

A lot of times we Christians like to make blanket confessions. "Forgive me for all my sins" we often say. Is there an argument for specific confession? 1 John 1:9 says, *If we confess our sins, he is faithful and just to forgive us our sins, and to cleanse us from all unrighteousness.*

The word confess in Greek is *homologeo* which means *to say the same thing and then to agree, admit, acknowledge[34]*. Please note that the tense of the word

---

34 Strong's Greek 3670

confess is the present tense. Our lives must be one of continuous confession of sin as they happen. This is not for our justification. That was done on the cross. Our confession is really repentance. It is identifying what is wrong, taking responsibility for our actions and accepting God's mercy and grace which has already been extend to us through Jesus Christ.

In addition, confession takes the wind out of the sails of the accuser. Just imagine that you are in a situation where someone is blackmailing you. A typical example would be if you are cheating on your spouse. If you choose to throw yourself at the mercy of your spouse and confess what you have done, would the accuser have any leverage against you again? David once said after being given a choice of punishment for his prideful sin of numbering Israel, that he would rather fall into the hands of God than that of man.

If we can come to the realization of what a merciful God we serve, then we will not be afraid to run to Him to access the forgiveness and mercy that He has provided for us. We would also not be so quick to be willfully disobedient, because we appreciate the love and mercy which, while freely available to us, was paid for with an innocent life for our sake.

Unconfessed sin

What happens when we let our sins go unconfessed? If we were living strictly according to law, we would be focused a myriad of punishments for our various sins.

He who covers his sin will not prosper, but whoever confesses and forsakes them will have mercy.[35]

By committing to getting married you will have taken to step necessary to forsake the sin of fornication. However, to have mercy requires two actions from us, confessing **AND** forsaking our sin. The responsibility is ours because mercy is already available to us.

In a way this reminds me of the four things that man must do in order for God

---

[35] Proverbs 28:13

to respond in 2 Chronicles 7:14 - *If My people who are called by my name*

- should humble themselves
- seek My face
- pray
- and turn from their wicked ways, **then**
- I will hear from heaven
- forgive their sins
- and heal their land.

The greater effort in seeking and receiving forgiveness is on us because God has already provided everything we need for life and godliness. You will notice my emphasis on the "if" and "then". In computer jargon, IF/THEN statements are conditional instructions to a software program. Basically it acts like a covenant - "If you do this, then this is the response." In the long run, all that we need is provided for us to walk in holiness and right living before God. Bear in mind however, that there is nothing we can do to "earn" our way into heaven. Obedience to God however, brings blessings.

Our lives demonstrate the choices that we make in our day to day spiritual walk. We can choose life or death, yet we are admonished to *"choose life."*

Transitioning From The Old Lifestyle

As I said previously, a common misconception about salvation is that once saved, everything is going to be alright. Wrong! Upon salvation, we have been pulled out of darkness into His marvelous light. With the attention of the enemy upon us, because we have chosen to walk a right path, we have to be extra vigilant and become aware of the various devices that he can use against us.

You are going to find yourself asking "What? Where is this coming from?" "How come I did not see this characteristic before?" Many questions will come - not the least of which is "Did we make a mistake getting married?" As a matter of fact, this question will come up many times. Do not entertain the thought. 2 Corinthians 10:5 says that we must be *"casting down imaginations, and every high thing, that exalts itself against the knowledge of God, bringing into captivity every thought to the obedience of Christ"*

Whereas in the past you might have dealt with difficulties "in the flesh", that is, with displays of temper, arguments, tears, emotional upheaval etc, now is the time to apply the Word to your marriage like never before - especially if you are saved. That must be your first resort. You will recall in the introduction, I referred to my temper. I rarely get in a rage, but when I did, epic proportions. When I am in a good mood, I cannot throw any missile in a straight line. Oh but when I got in a rage, I would bean you in a minute!

I still get "teary" when I am upset, but I do not fly into a rage anymore. Thank you Lord for working out the fruits[36] of the Spirit in me. As I learned to apply the Word to my life and to our marriage, the rage episodes became less and less until they no longer happen. I have learned to put a bit and bridle on my tongue so that even when Rohan says

---

[36] Galatians 5:22??

hurtful things, I never respond. Proverbs 26:20 says that *without wood a fire goes out.* Instead, I wait until we are both calm and attempt to present my point of view at that time. Those who have known me from early days, know that this is a far cry from who I used to be.

A teacher at the Bible College I attended, Apostle Bishop, in teaching about relationships, said that with Jesus at the center, one of us has to stay close to the center so that the other can find their way back. When both of us move away from the center (Jesus), it is difficult for us both to come back to where we should be. If one of us stays close to Jesus, then the other in searching for Jesus, in trying to reconnect with Him in a meaningful way, will find the other.

Transition from our old lifestyle is only lasting with a constant application of the Word. This means that every aspect of our lives must be surrendered to God, to the lordship of Jesus Christ. It means letting go of our idols, including, believe it or not, our marriage. I know it seems strange that our marriages can become our idol but believe me, it can. Anything that we place above God is an idol.

Ask the Holy Spirit to reveal to you the ways in which your marriage has become your idol. Use your journal to record this and ask Him to tell you what to do and how.

I had reached this place in my marriage to Rohan. Since writing this book, I have arrived at my Mount Moriah in this regard. I have had to come to the place where I have no choice but to trust God completely with our marriage. I had to let it go completely and hand it over to Him. Every time, I am tempted to fix something, I remember that it is no longer mine to fix. He will heal all the rifts, the wounds, the pains.

The Word brings healing, redemption, renewal and transformation of the mind. Apply liberally as many times per day as you wish.

The covenant that came into effect when Jesus was crucified, buried and resurrected gives us the way to redemption. Confession of our sin brings about forgiveness and sanctification.[1 John 1:9]

This covenant cancelled our past as surely as wind blows away chaff. So how do we transition from the old life to the new?

In the scenario of Rohan and myself, I was a Christian living in sin (willfully) and he was not saved until we actually went for counseling. Once I confessed the sin of fornication my forgiveness was automatic. The scripture does not say anywhere that the forgiveness of the sin we committed would take a few days to be absolved.

However we (especially I) lived under the bondage of law. I believe also that as the more mature Christian, I might have led him astray by my actions. Thank God for mercy.

The battlefield is in the mind. There is no doubt about it. Conformity to the Word brings about renewal of the mind. When, with the help of my mentor, I began to apply the Word to my thoughts, I was finally freed of a lot of things that I was struggling with in my mind.

It was a little weird for me to realize that I could apply the Word to my thoughts. What I mean is that I had an head knowledge of it, but the reality of it did not connect in my heart. We often apply the Word to our actions, but rarely our thought life. Our enemy takes advantage of this and runs rampant throughout our thought life and we struggle incessantly.

There is no part of our life where we should not apply the Word. This is what is entailed in complete surrendering of our will to God. As we go through each day, applying the Word to every thought (vain imagination) that dares to challenge the knowledge of God in our lives, we move further and further away from the old lifestyle into the new.

Chapter Seven: Can We Survive The Onslaught?

If we examine our relationship with God, we will find that same attitude mirrored in our human relationship of marriage. For example, one partner may be constantly working at their relationship with God. They seek out time with Him, speak to Him constantly, sing to Him etc., while the other partner might be of the opinion that once they are saved, there is no need to go to church, no need to do Bible study or any such thing. You will find that the partner who constantly seeks the presence of God wants also the presence of their spouse, while the other is not even aware of a disconnect in the relationship.

Satan is out to destroy marriages especially, I believe, because God so ordained. The scripture says that he is like a roaring lion, who comes to steal, kill and destroy. Remember too, that Satan is subtlety itself. He is not likely to come with the obvious. The diligent couple who continuously seek the presence of God together will be made aware of the plans of the enemy.

When only one person is pressing in though, it is that much harder to overcome as a unit. The result is that couples are often blind-sided by the enemy and end up asking "where in heaven's name did that come from?" Or, depending on which fruit of the spirit is not in operation, the response might be more colorful. As individuals as well as a unit, couples have to be proactive in the protection of the sanctity of their marriage. We have to learn to "see the wind" not just the effects. If a pervasive weed is growing in your garden, simply pulling out the leaves will not solve the problem. You have to determine to get to the root and pull it out completely. The only way to get to a root, is to soak the soil with water (the Word) and dig. This means probing into some uncomfortable places in our lives. It means facing some ugly truths and giants, but the end result of deliverance and freedom from oppression is worth it.

Some probing questions would be - are there trust issues? Why? Is this a new thing? What changed to bring about the erosion of trust? These are the questions that we must ask and face the answers no matter how difficult. I reiterate, that only in facing truth, can we adequately deal with the everyday issues of our lives.

There will be times when you feel as if there is no rest. As soon as one fire is put out, another comes up. What is blowing the sparks to where the fire starts? Can we come into agreement that when a situation comes up that causes division, that we first face the issue in prayer? If our solutions are not coming from God, they will most likely cause further deterioration in the relationship. Can we agree to get our emotions in control and agree that it is not about what we feel, but what the Word of God says that must prevail? Does our emotional response agree with the Word? If not, we are on the wrong path.

Are we willing to take responsibility for our actions? Will we be like that couple in the Garden that sought to shift blame from themselves? Do we seek to position ourselves and our marriages in God? This is the only way to not just survive but thrive in the face of the onslaught of the enemy's attacks. What of our children? What are we teaching them when they see us buckling under the strain of the onslaught of Satan? What are we demonstrating about faith? When we teach our children by demonstration that we are to take everything to the Lord in prayer we are setting a firm foundation in their lives. If my grandchildren ever see me crying, their first question to me after asking me what's wrong is "grandma did you pray?" My answer had better be yes, or I am going to have to explain why.

Wives, you will be held responsible for not showing respect to your husbands. Respect includes not gossiping about him to your friends, not being receptive to gossip about him either. Respect also includes not shouting at him, even if he is shouting at you, etc. Respect means holding your position in the Word despite your temptation to retaliate.

Husbands, you will be held accountable for not loving your wives as Christ loved the church, for not standing up in your authoritative position. Is your wife sick? Have you prayed for her healing? I had a headache once that lasted for about a week. I prayed and prayed and still it would not go away. I asked the Lord what to do and He said "ask your husband to pray for you." I did and Rohan, (not being much of a talker) made a declaration in Jesus' name and five minutes later - no headache. Are you taking authority of the situations that arise in your family, or are you just letting things slide? Are you the first to make amends even though you may not be at fault? (This question is also directed at wives).

Your respective positions are not dependent upon the actions of your partners. Recently Rohan and I had a very big disagreement. During that time, although he was being quite disrespectful (using expletives), I never once retaliated in like manner. I still insisted on praying with him when he was leaving for his work. I told him a few days later that I had forgiven him, despite him not apologising, because my forgiveness of his actions is not dependent on his repentance. While we were yet Jesus' enemies, he died for us. How could I do less?

The focus of your marriage is not what you as an individual can get out of it. It must always be about how can I help / uplift my partner? Focus on self is a satanic expression. Remember the five "I will's" in Isaiah 14:13. Satan's focus was always, "I will." Yet, when God was creating man He said "let us". When we left our parents and cleaved together to become one, it was no longer about each of us as individuals, but about us as a unit.

Are you the focus of your marriage?

Another consideration is counseling. Always seek guidance. Remember to seek to get this counseling from your pastor, or a Christian married couple whom you respect. Even if your spouse will not go, you be sure to go ahead and receive some good counseling in the Word. This will help to strengthen you as you labour in prayer for your spouse.

How attacks gain entrance

Attacks against a marriage come in many forms. I have alluded to some things already in various chapters, but it bears repeating:

Gossiping - This is not an affliction that is only common to women. I have heard men gossip together in such a way that many women would cringe. There is no excuse - it just should not be done. The couple must see their marriage as sacred and as such discussions about the very private issues must be in a setting where a solution can be found. A good barometer is the question - "will what I am about to say uplift my spouse or find a solution to the problems we are having?" If the answer is no, then don't say it.

The toxic friends/ family. They do not like your spouse. They do everything to turn your mind from him/her. They never have nothing good to say, and that is usually demonstrated in how quick they are to suggest negative things including calling your spouse names. I am not saying you are to disown them or bear them malice, but you have to make the determination that they are toxic to your marriage and love them from afar.

Your family or friends should never be given the opportunity to believe that they can come between you and your spouse. Family especially, should never be given the opportunity to feel that they can make plans with you about your life without including your spouse. Remember when you came together, you left mother and father and cleaved to your spouse - you are now a unit and must present yourselves as one at all times.

Best friends of the opposite sex - No, I am not saying you cannot have a close friend of the opposite sex, but that person is no longer your best friend. Your closest friend should be the person that you are married to. (Refer to questionnaire). This is a recipe for trouble if there ever was one. I have been blessed with some really great "big brothers". These men of God in my life are the people to whom I turn when I want a male perspective on stuff (whether in my marriage or otherwise). However, I never present an issue to anyone of them on a one to one basis. (Before I was married - certainly). Instead, I will gather two out of the four of them and present my case. Having their input has proven valuable to me. I also never meet them at their homes - especially if it will be just the two of us alone. There are hugs aplenty to go around, yet you will never find anyone of them and me in a corner hugging. In other words, my interaction with them has to be more circumspect especially now that I am married. It is just too easy for the enemy to setup.

Consider the scenario: *I am facing difficulties in my marriage and I keep confiding to this one person about issues between my husband and I. This person now becomes the "go to" person to talk to when I am having issues with my husband. Before you know it I am no longer communicating with my husband, but to this person. One day, I am crying on his shoulder and he is hugging me and next thing you know we are kissing. Before you know it we are having sex.* I know I mentioned this scenario elsewhere in the book but it bears repeating. **Why make it so easy for the enemy?** Be vigilant and remember the enemy is subtlety itself.

Unwholesome conversations - As strange as this may seem, having unwholesome conversations is yet another pitfall for you and spells disaster for your marriage. Ask yourself what types of conversations you are entertaining.

Recently I was walking in my community and a young man made a comment to me about my body. I immediately confronted him and asked why he thought that I would want to have that conversation with him. I was not smiling but very stern. Eventually he apologised.

On another occasion, one of Rohan's friends made a comment about my breasts. I not only made him realize that I was not pleased by his presumption, but he was swift to apologise when he realized that I was about to call Rohan on the phone.

A young lady in the community, asked me once, why I always wore a wrap skirt whenever I wore tights. She said that since I looked so good, I should "show off the things." I told her that what is for my husband is not for everyone else to see.

Men are also on the receiving end of this. While all of this attention may seem flattering, remember that flattery is really about getting you to lower our guard and your response determines the next action of the flatterer. When does it stop? We really should refrain from idle, unwholesome talk.

Not carrying yourself well - I know this sounds odd. Consider this, you leave the house looking like you are not being cared for, looking unkempt. Along comes someone of the opposite sex who decides to "fix you up" because obviously your man/woman does not know how to take care of you. The next thing you know, you are comparing the treatment that you are getting to the one you do not seem to be getting at home and you become vulnerable to this person.

Your value system should be of such, that (a) you dress as the "royal priesthood" that you are, (b) you recognize that how you look determines how people see your spouse because you represent them, and finally, (c) you should never accept gifts that you cannot tell your spouse about.

These are but a few instances of how attacks against marriage gain entrance. I am sure that if you examine your situation, you can find a few more examples. The important thing to remember here is that if the Holy Spirit shows you where there is an open door, He is giving you an opportunity to shut it.

Chapter Eight: The Couple That Prays Together

You have heard it said many times, "The family that prays together, stays together." When a couple makes the time to pray together mountains are moved in that family. Praying couples are in the right positioning to receive from God, because they seek the face of God together. The Holy Spirit is attracted to unity. He does great and mighty things, demonstrating His power when we are united. Not only should they pray together, in accordance with the edict to "pray without ceasing", they should pray for each other individually also.

There is nothing like the Word of God to activate angels to move on our behalf. The scripture says that angels harken to the voice of the Word of God. A praying couple becomes a powerhouse when they study the Word together. They are able to speak the promises of God over each other's lives and the lives of their children.

The importance of corporate devotional time before God cannot be over emphasized. This time of worshiping and studying the Word together goes a long way to strengthening a marriage. This is one of the areas I would definitely like to see strengthened in our (Rohan & I) marriage. I am counting my blessings though, at least he does not leave the house, whether it is to go hunting or fishing, without us praying for each other. Yet, I will admit to wanting to see us both go deeper with God.

We (Christian couples) cannot cease to pray for our spouses and marriages in general. James says that we ask and do not receive because we ask amiss. How do you pray for your spouse? Are you telling God of all the problems you are facing?

I remember a friend of mine who is a young wife, came to me one day and was telling me of all the problems she was facing with her husband. I advised her to pray and she insisted that she did. When I asked her to demonstrate, it was exactly as I suspected. She was praying the problem. A principle that is constantly lost on us is that what we speak is what comes to life. We are made in the image and likeness of God, who created the world by the declarations from His mouth. He said "let there be" and there was. It stands to reason that whatever we declare is what will be. I told my friend about an incident that happened to me:

I was up one night and I was praying before going to bed. I thought that Rohan was asleep. I knelt in my bed and said "Lord, I thank You that Rohan is a righteous man. I thank You, that he does not sit with the scornful, not stand with sinners. I thank You that his delight is in You. I thank You that he will meditate on Your Word day and night and delight in it." I said Amen and went to sleep. About 10 minutes later, I felt his arm come around my waist and he whispered "thanks" and continued with his snoring.

I instructed my friend even as I am instructing you now, **pray out loud the solution**. God is already aware of the

122

problems. You do not need to tell Him anything He already knows. We have been given the authority to represent Him and speak His Word into every situation of our lives. In the final section of this book I will demonstrate with a few scriptures how to do this for some of the various situations we face. We must come to the place where we recognize that every part of the Scripture is for us, and we can insert names where we see a verse that speaks to a situation in our lives.

Husband's Prayer of Repentance

Heavenly Father, I come before you a broken man ready to confess my sins and turn away from them. I realize that I have misused my divine authority and spoken negatively over the lives of my wife and children. I have not supported my family emotionally, spiritually or financially, and I have abused their trust. I have done wickedly by being unfaithful to my wife, given myself over to addictions, sexual, gambling, drugs and [add any other that you think applies to you].

But You O God are a merciful God, slow to anger and quick to forgive. Thank You for the Blood of Jesus which washes away all my iniquities and my transgressions. I surrender myself to the Holy Spirit to guide me in the way of truth. Keep my feet ever on the path that you have set for me and order my steps in Your Way only. I will meditate on Your Word day and night and it shall ever be upon my lips. Thank You for grace and mercy and for the provision that you have made with the finished work of the Cross. Let the words of my mouth and the meditation of my heart be acceptable to You, O Lord my Strength and Redeemer. In Jesus' Name, let Your will be done in my life. Amen

Wife's Prayer of Repentance

My Heavenly Father, I come before you a broken woman, confessing my sins and forsaking my former ways. I come to access the forgiveness that You provided for me through the finished work of the Cross.

I confess to gossiping, not being industrious and not showing respect to my husband. I confess to rebellion and staging a coup when I saw that he was not in his rightful place as priest of this house, instead of praying for his return to his rightful place. I confess to being nagging, badgering and being quarrelsome. I confess to neglecting the welfare of the household, being financial irresponsible, giving myself over to addictions, - sexual, gambling [add any other that applies to you].

But You O God are a merciful God, slow to anger and quick to forgive. Thank You for the Blood of Jesus which washes away all my iniquities and my transgressions. I surrender myself to the Holy Spirit to guide me in the way of truth. Teach me to place a bit and bridle on my tongue, so that I will not start any fires. As I submit to the authority of Your Word, teach me to have a submissive heart before my husband. Tune in my ears to the frequency of the

Holy Spirit who guides me into all truth.
In Jesus' Name. Amen

Praying God's Word Over Your Spouse

Thank You Lord that _____ is
blessed because he/she does not operate
in agreement with the wicked and
scornful. Thank You that he/she delights
in Your Word and meditates on it day
and night. Thank You that he/she is
fruitful, well-watered, with his/her roots
sunk deeply in You and whatever he/she
does will prosper.

I bless Your Name Lord because
_____ is not of the ungodly, but
a righteous man/woman, he/she is able
to stand in Your judgement and in the
congregation of the righteous, and shall
not perish.
_____ can enter into the
hill of the Lord and stand in Your holy
place because the works of his/her hands
are righteous, his/her heart is sold out to
you and seeking after Your
righteousness, he/she is not prideful, has
not given himself/herself over to the lust
of the eyes, the pride of life, and lusts of
the flesh, nor has he/she defiled his/her

lips with lies. I declare that he/she is of the generation that constantly seeks Your face and the Kingdom of Heaven has come to him/her.

I declare that he/she is able to receive the blessings of the Lord. I declare that he/she will lift up his/her head in praise at all times and in all situations and circumstances so that You, the King of Glory, the Lord mighty in battle, the God of his/her salvation can manifest mightily in his/her life. In Jesus' name, Amen.

(Adapted from Psalm 1 and Psalm 24)

Wife's Prayer For Her Husband

Father, in the name of Jesus I declare the following over the life of my husband _____:

- That he loves me and is not bitter against me,
- That because he honors me, his prayers are not hindered,
- That he loves me as You love the church
- That he is not a denier of the faith and he is better than an infidel, because he provides for his own house,

- That he lives joyfully with me and loves me all the days that you have given him under the sun,
- That he has made a covenant with his eyes not to look lustfully at another woman,
- That he is my authority in the home just as Jesus is the authority of the church,
- That he will not dealt treacherously with me so that You will not be a witness against him,
- That he is industrious and blessed with divine ideas to make him prosperous,
- That he knows Your voice when he hears it,
- That he recognizes that I am bone of his bone and flesh of his flesh,
- That he is better to me than ten sons,
- That the plans You have for him cannot fail and he lives in accordance with those plans,
- That You will bless the work of his hands,
- That he is a good steward of Your provisions for us,
- That he is quick to forgive,
- That he is quick to repent,
- That he is not hard hearted,
- That he is patient and full of peace,
- That he has a humble teachable spirit,

- That he will grow in the Word by diligent study,
- That he will boldly declare the truth of the Gospel of Jesus Christ to his peers,
- That his past no longer determines his future because he is a new creation in Jesus Christ,
- That his health will prosper as his soul prospers,
- That he will appropriate every promise that you have ever made for him in Your Word,
- That his desire is always to seek Your face,
- That he never stops praying for my welfare and the welfare of our marriage
- That he outdoes me in showing honor
- I declare that this is the truth of his life in Jesus' name, Amen.

Husband's Prayer For His Wife

Father, in the name of Jesus, I thank you that I have found an excellent wife in _____ who is far more precious than jewels. I declare the following over her life:

- That she does me good and not harm
- That she works with willing hands

- That she has a mind for business and is a good steward over what you have provided for us
- That she never stops praying for my welfare and the welfare of our marriage
- That she is skilled with many talents
- That she is generous of spirit and willing to help those less fortunate
- That I can call her blessed
- That she fears the Lord and the glory of the Lord is upon her
- That her works praise her
- That she is respectful
- That she does not eat the bread of idleness
- That she has made a covenant with her eyes not to look lustfully at another man
- That my heart can trust her
- That because I have her, I have found favor from You
- That she is my crown and does not bring shame to me
- That she builds the home and not tea it down
- That she is slow to anger, slow to speak and quick to hear
- That she upholds our marriage in honor
- That she is not quarrelsome
- That she will not bear the curses of the pains of childbirth

- That because of her uprightness, the adversary has no occasion to bring slander against her or our home
- That she outdoes me in showing honor
- That the plans You have for her cannot fail and she lives in accordance with those plans,
- That You will bless the work of her hands,
- That she is quick to forgive,
- That she is quick to repent,
- That she is not hard hearted,
- That she is patient and full of peace,
- That she has a humble teachable spirit,
- That she will grow in the Word by diligent study,
- That she will boldly declare the truth of the Gospel of Jesus Christ to her peers,
- That her past no longer determines her future because she is a new creation in Jesus Christ,
- That her health will prosper as her soul prospers,
- That she will appropriate every promise that you have ever made for her in Your Word,
- That her desire is always to seek Your face,

I declare that this is the truth of her life in Jesus' name, Amen

Declarations About Intimacy

Father, in the name of Jesus, we declare the following over our intimate life with each other:

- That our life of intimacy with each reflects our lives of intimacy with You
- That we satisfy each other and are captivated by each other's love
- That our fountains are blessed as we rejoice in each other
- That You have made us one with a portion of the Spirit in our union.
- That we encourage each other and build each other up
- That we drink water only from each other's well
- That our countenance is lovely to each other
- That we are the beloved of each other
- That our love for each other is like lilies among thorns
- That we desire each other's love more than we desire the things of this world and our desire is only towards each other
- That the garden of our love is sealed to outsiders. It is a well of

living waters from which we drink abundantly.
- That we shall eat of the pleasant fruits of our garden
- That our hearts are sealed, our love cannot be quenched, nor can floods drown it.

This we declare to be the truth for intimacy in our marriage, in Jesus's name. Amen

Prologue

I have been obedient to the Lord and laid out all that he has spoken to me. It is my fervent prayer that this book will be a blessing to you, your spouse and your marriage. The prayers that have been included are simply examples of how you can use the scriptures to speak into your circumstances.

This book is for you if you are married, planning to get married or single with thought of finding a spouse.

I ask that you be kind enough to leave a review when you are finished and, if you have found this book useful and it ministered to you, that you share / recommend it to someone else.

Once again, I thank you for taking the time to read this book. May the Lord bless you and keep you.

With a heart of love

Sylvia M Dallas

Excerpt from <u>AND THE PRISONERS</u> <u>HEARD THEM - Your Life of Praise Can</u> <u>Bring Freedom to Others</u> [Sylvia M Dallas] (ISBN : 978-976-95691-2-6 [ebook], 978-976-95691-1-9 (paperback)

AND THE PRISONERS HEARD THEM

"And at midnight, Paul and Silas prayed and sang praises unto God: and the prisoners heard them" – Acts 16:25 KJV

Picture this. You are an unsaved person, and you keep hearing about this God that brings joy, peace and love. You have friends who say that they are Christians but you have yet to see any evidence of joy in their lives. All you can hear about is how difficult life is, they hardly ever smile and never have anything positive to say. Why on earth would you want to embrace the Christian life if this is the evidence of it?

As Christians we are supposed to be evangelizing, going out into the world and making disciples of all men according to the instructions we received in the Great Commission.[3] This means we are to preach the good news of the Gospel and drawing people to Christ. How can we achieve what is required of us if our spirits are downcast, if our countenance is

---

[3] Matthew 28: 19-20 KJV

low? Would you be attracted to the lifestyle of the person above? I think not!

Paul and Silas after being accused were locked in the deepest part of the dungeon and this was after they had just had "many stripes laid upon them " and "their feet fast in stocks"[4]. So beaten, placed in the inner part of the prison with their feet made immovable, they did the most unlikely thing...they began to pray and out of their prayers came praises which they sang unto God, doing the very thing for which they were jailed.

So you are in the dungeon, experiencing the similar conditions and a strange sound reaches your ears. "Who in their right mind could be singing in this place, at this time of the night?" "Are they aware that this is a prison?" "Isn't that sound coming from the innermost part of the prison where the worst punishment takes place?" Here you are in your most miserable of conditions and someone in a worst position is singing? At first, you would probably wonder if the conditions they are experiencing have gotten to their heads. As you listen, you realize this is not the crazy maniacal sound of someone slowly going off their rocker. This is pure unadulterated joy.

You cannot understand it, but as the sound penetrates your mind, it touches something deep inside of you and you listen. You want to catch the rhythm. Suddenly you find yourself swaying to the beat. You

---

[4] Acts 16:22-24 KJV

don't know the song but deep down something bubbles up inside of you. You feel as if there is a foaming fountain coming up from within your belly. As you continue to listen, a shout escapes you, you become somehow involved in what is happening and you feel tremors. Something earth shaking, soul shaking is taking place. You don't know what it is. You have never experienced anything like this before, but you definitely feel it and you know change is coming. Suddenly your chains are loosed, broken off of you, fallen to the ground.

Your praises to God are not just for you. Your praises need to be heard by others to bring deliverance to them. The praises to God from you cannot remain in your thoughts, they must come from the utterance of your lips to bring change to someone's life – not just yours. At the midnight of your life, beaten and chained to immovability, when you think that you are at rock bottom, you have no idea where the next meal is coming from, how you are going to make it the next day, facing life or death surgery, facing deathlike situations – trust God and praise Him.

Your praises can bring about the greatest move of evangelism in your life. Trials are always an opportunity to demonstrate God's power. When someone who is not saved sees you praising your way through your situations, sees you feeding yourself with the Word, sees the manifestation of God's peace in your life, they see you sleeping, unmoved by the storm and they wonder "how can I get some of that peace?" They move from "how can I" to "I want", and before

137

you know it you are being asked "where do you go to church?"

Years ago, I went to visit a friend at her home. As the day passed and I was enjoying my time with her, there was a knock on the door. When she answered, there were about five policemen with a search warrant. I was told that I could not leave, nor was I allowed to make any calls. Well I just simply turned around, lay down on the carpet and went to sleep. This was not a restless, tossing and turning kind of sleep. This was deep comfortable, snoring kind of sleep. I woke up periodically and they were still there every time I woke up. The last time I woke up, one of the policemen asked me how come I am able to sleep. I told him that I was at peace because I know I was not involved in anything. He allowed me to leave.

When you praise, you are at rest. All the encumbrances become loosed from your life and the enemy can find nothing in you.

"And suddenly there was a great earthquake, so that the foundations of the prison were shaken; and immediately all the doors were opened, and everyone's bands were loosed." - Acts 16:26 KJV

Excerpts from Sylvia's new book of poetry - THE RIGHT KIND OF INTIMACY - For God Has Me (ISBN : 978-976-95691-5-7 [ebook], 978-976-95691-4-0 (paperback)

Love Encounter

My heart quickens
It feels as if it would burst
So overcome with passion
Wrought from an encounter with You

I lean into your embrace
As I rest my head
Upon Your bosom
The sound of Your heartbeats
Echoes
Reverberates
Like thunder

I feel
Vibrations
Pulsing
Throughout my body
And even into my spirit
As our heartbeats
Find a unified rhythm

Coming into agreement
Of a great union with You
My soul knows very well
It's real

It's trustworthy
This outpouring of love
From Your heart to mine

My spirit has caught on
To a divine rhythm
I am ruined for any other sound
Any other beat
I can never be the same again.

Come & See

I heard Him speak
And followed Him
And when He asked me
What was it that I sought
I said "Lord, show me where You live "
He said
"Come and see "

And I obeyed.

My joy in His presence
Could not be contained
I went seeking a friend
With whom to share
When I saw him I said
"I have found the Christ
Come and see "

I saw another friend
Who told me about Him
He said his heart listened

When Jesus said "Follow me "
And together we went
And told other friends
"We have found a
Good thing out of Nazareth

Come and see "
They who went to see Him

Realized that He already knew them
And each went to a friend
And proclaimed
"We have found Him
Who knew us
Him who redeemed us
Him who promised us
Open heavens because we believed

We found Him
Who stormed the gates of hell
And took back the keys!
Who heals the sick
Him who frees the oppressed
We have found Him
Who stills the storm
Walks on water
We have found Him!
We have found Him!
Come and see!"

About the Author

Sylvia M Dallas, born June 9, 1965 accepted Jesus Christ as her Lord and Saviour at the age of 10 years. It was at that time that she discovered her gift for writing. In 2000 she published her first book under the pseudonym Gina Rey Forest and several books later on. In 2007 she declared unto God, "I will not perform on stage again, or write another poem unless it glorifies You". She was immediately tested. She received several offers to perform her previous style of sensuous poetry with pay. She turned them all down. In 2011, she recommitted her life to God, promising to be obedient to His word and the promptings of His Holy Spirit. This is her third book since January 2014. She has been married to Rohan Dallas since 2011.

For feedback on this book you may contact her at: sylvia@sylviadallas.com. Twitter: @syldallas
Facebook: www.facebook.com/sylviamdallas or visit her blog THE BETTER DIRECTION at http://sylviadallas.com
Telephone: (876) 782-1866

www.ingramcontent.com/pod-product-compliance
Lightning Source LLC
Chambersburg PA
CBHW071857020426
42331CB00010B/2549